www.cuillandre.com
hcuillandre@yahoo.fr

ISBN: 978-1-84728-272-9

Elsewhere

Hervé Cuillandre

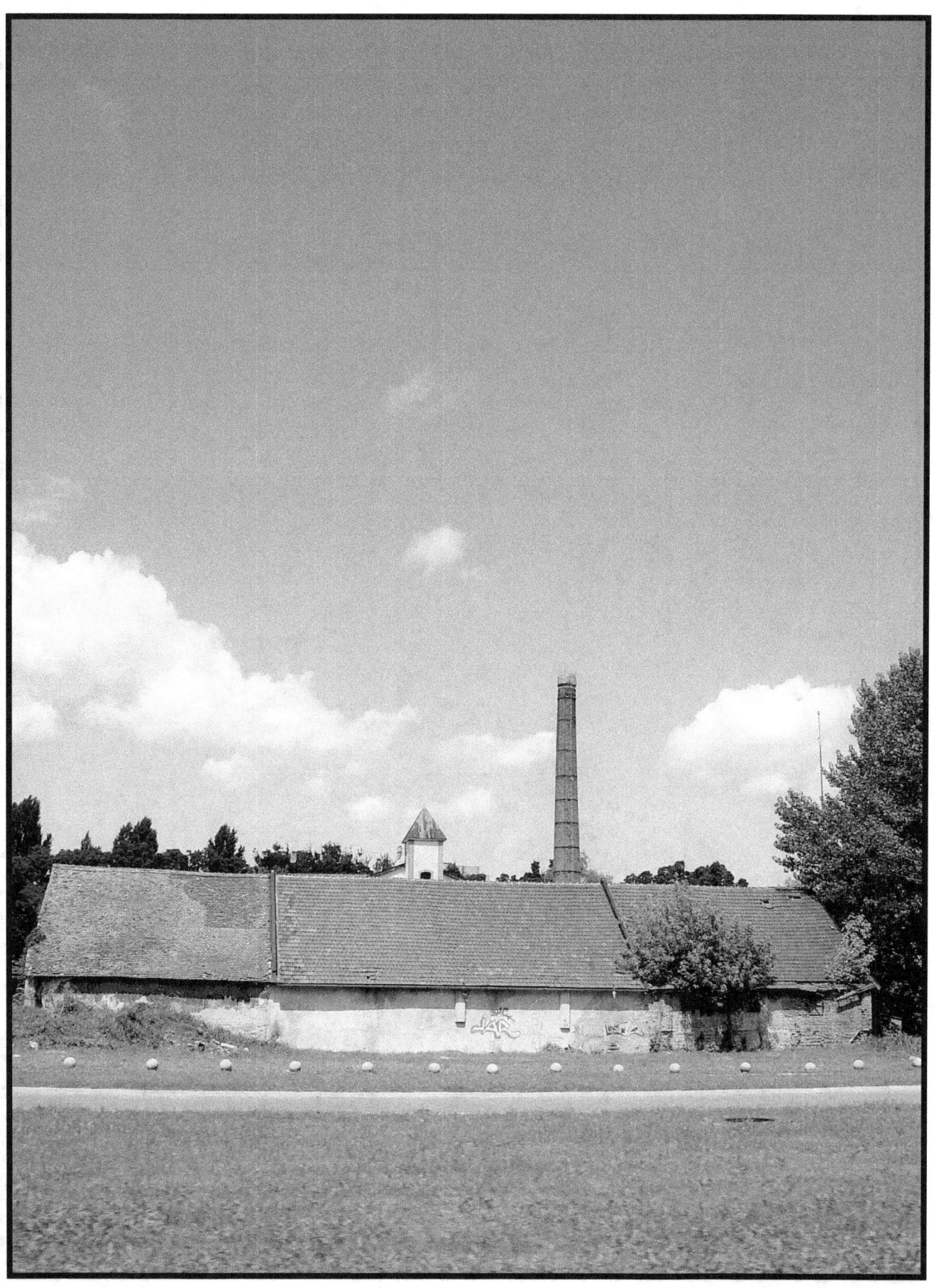

Novi Sad (Serbia) – August 2006

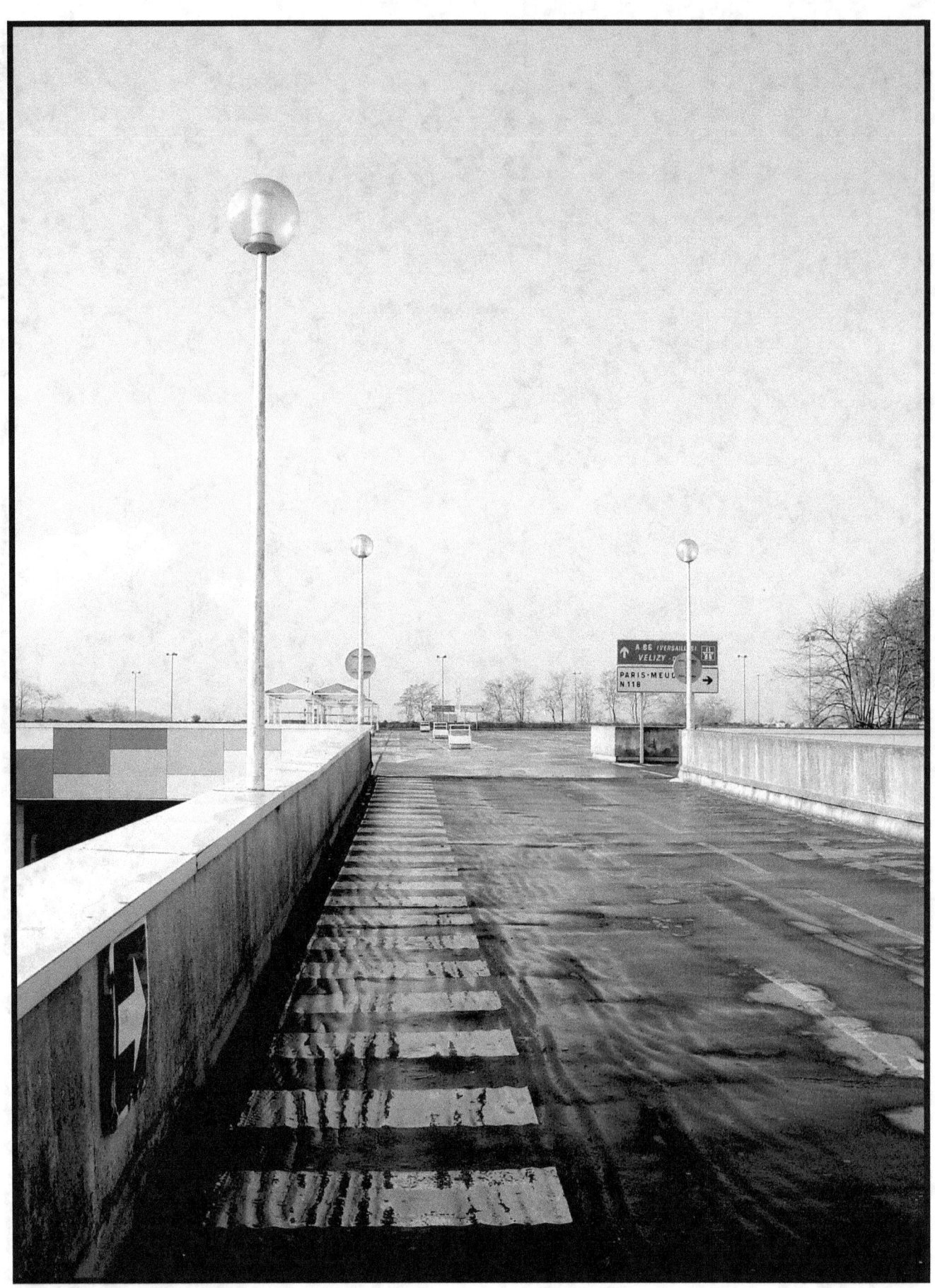

Vélizy (France) – April 2004

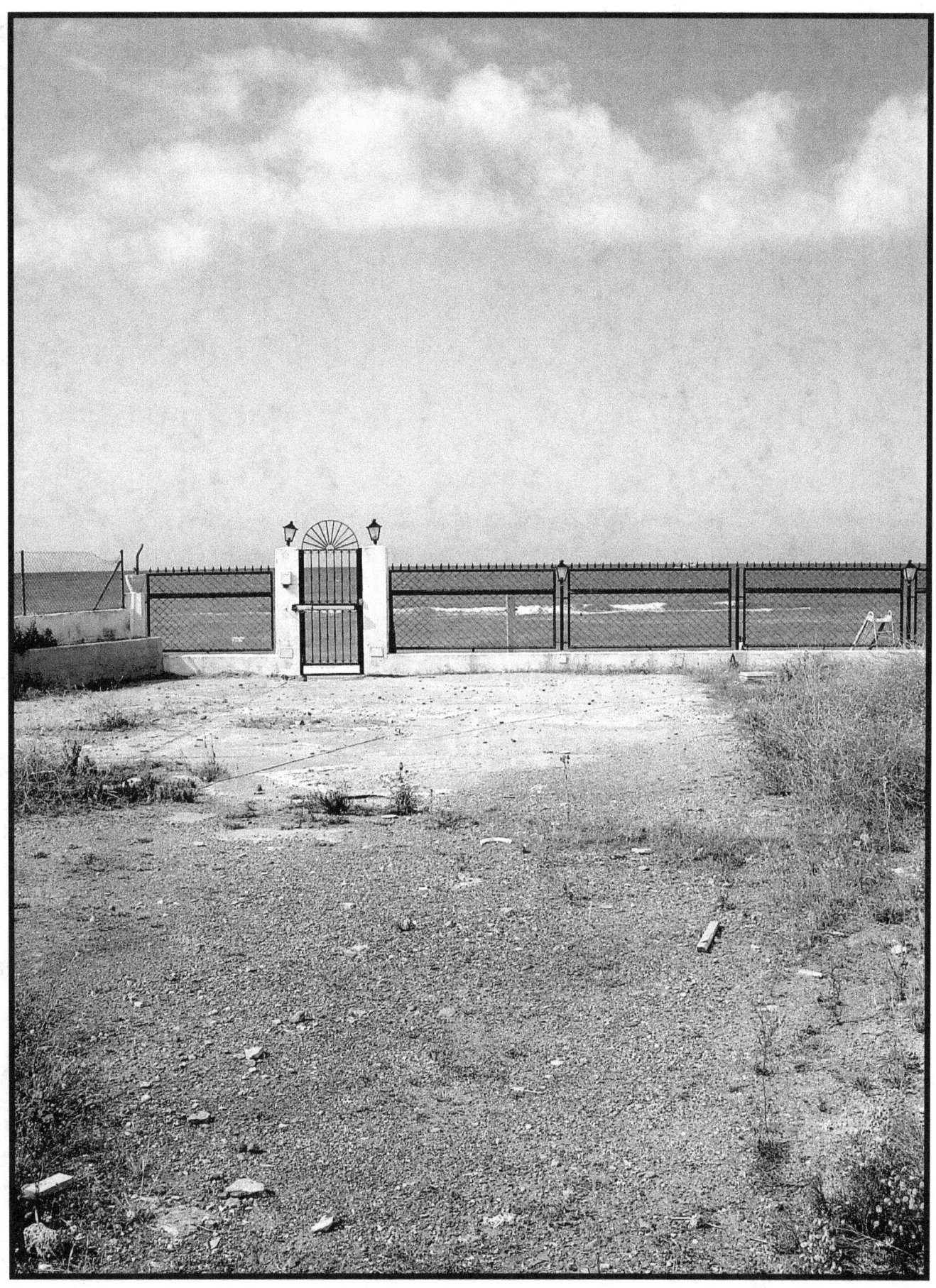

Marbella (Spain) – June 2004

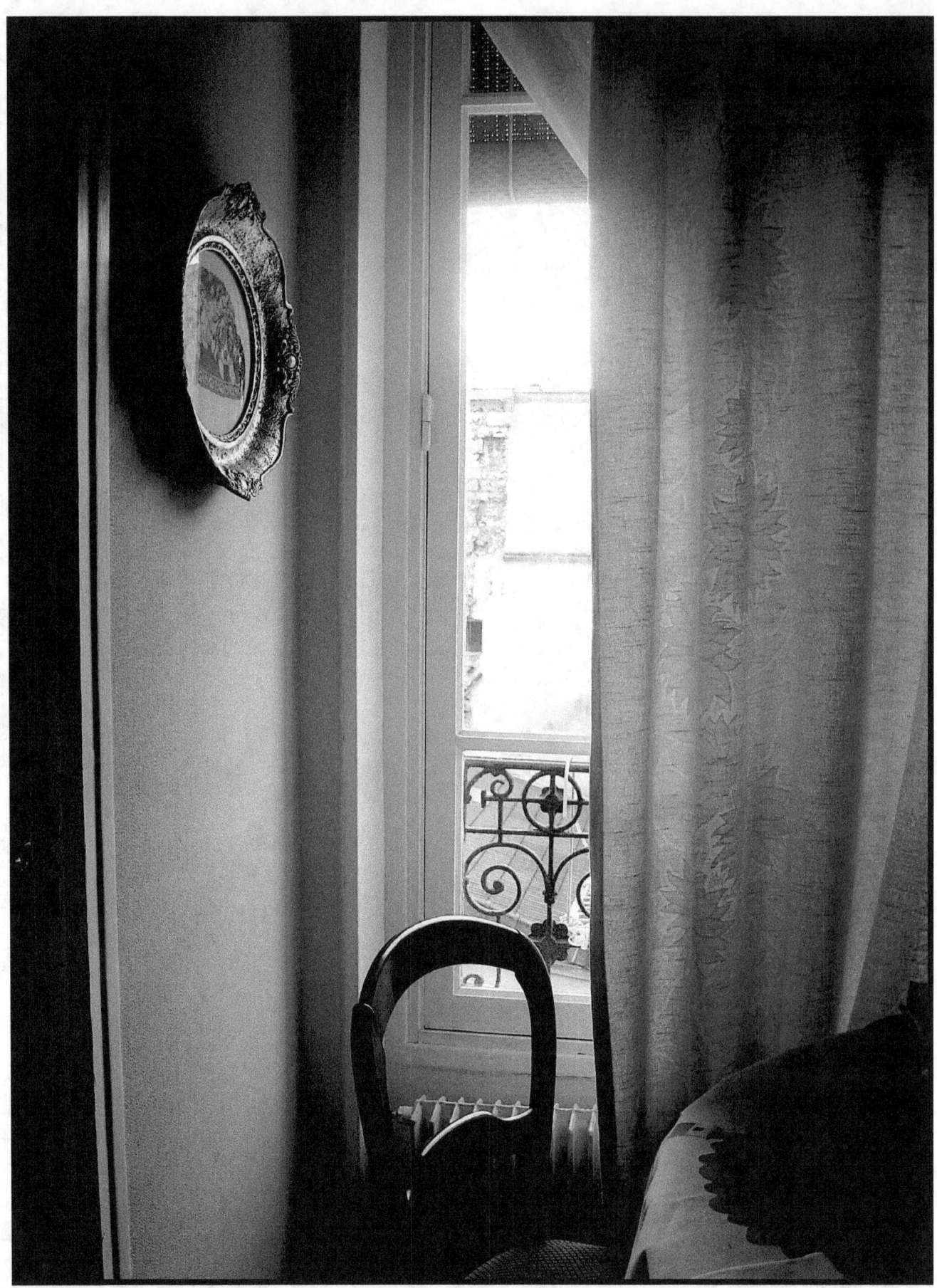

Paris (France) – January 2006

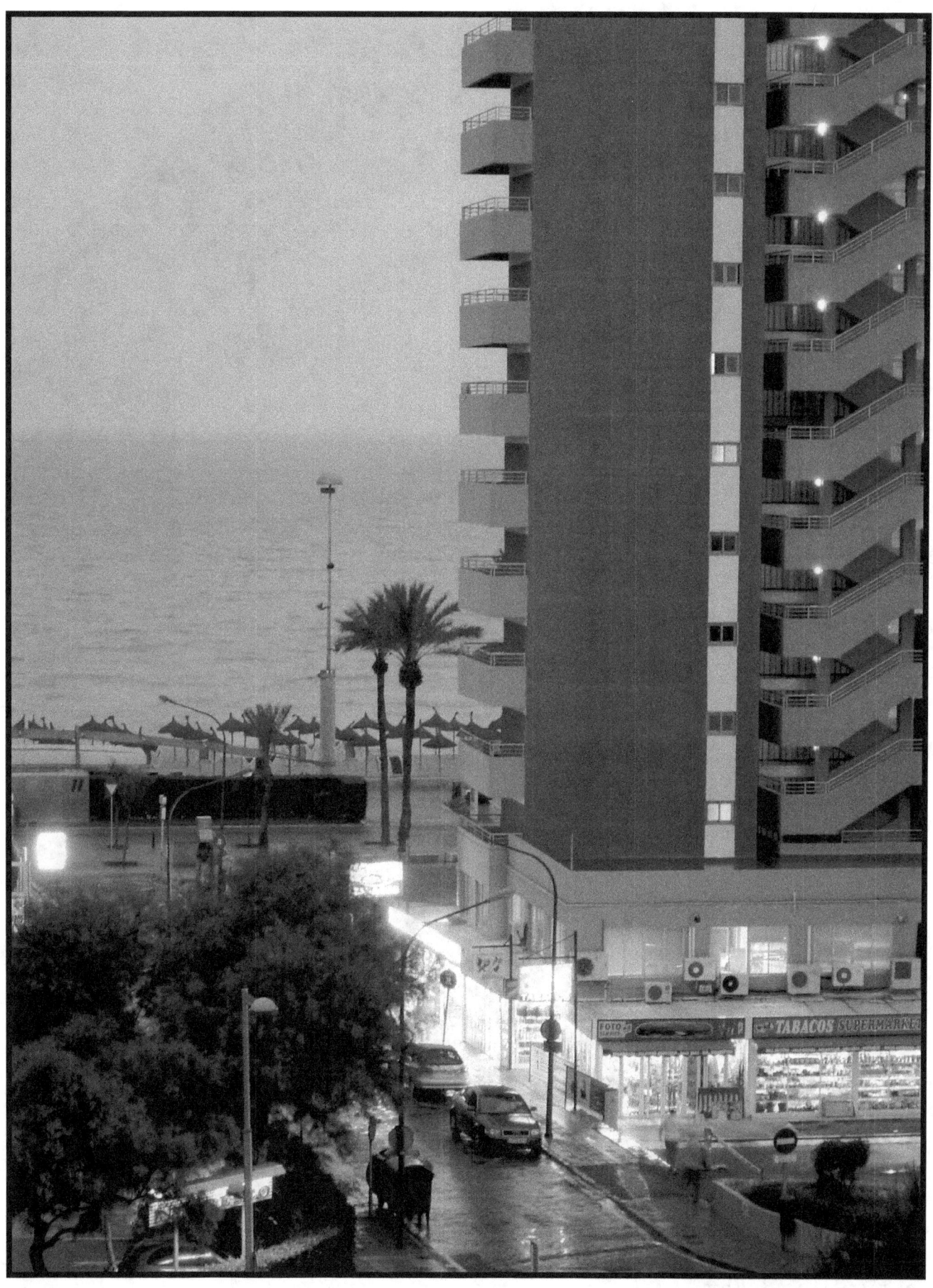

Mallorca (Spain) – June 2006

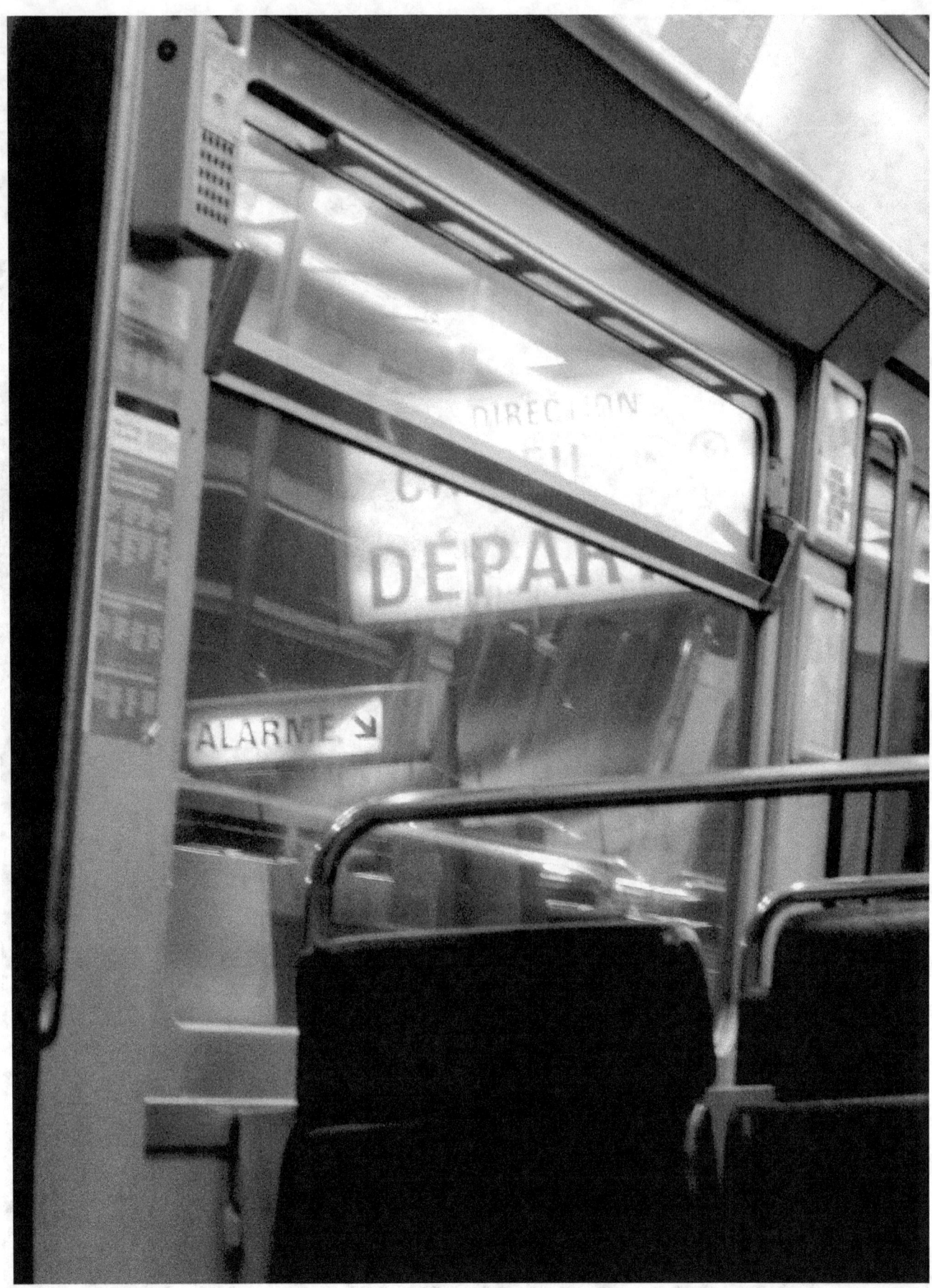

Paris (France) – April 2004

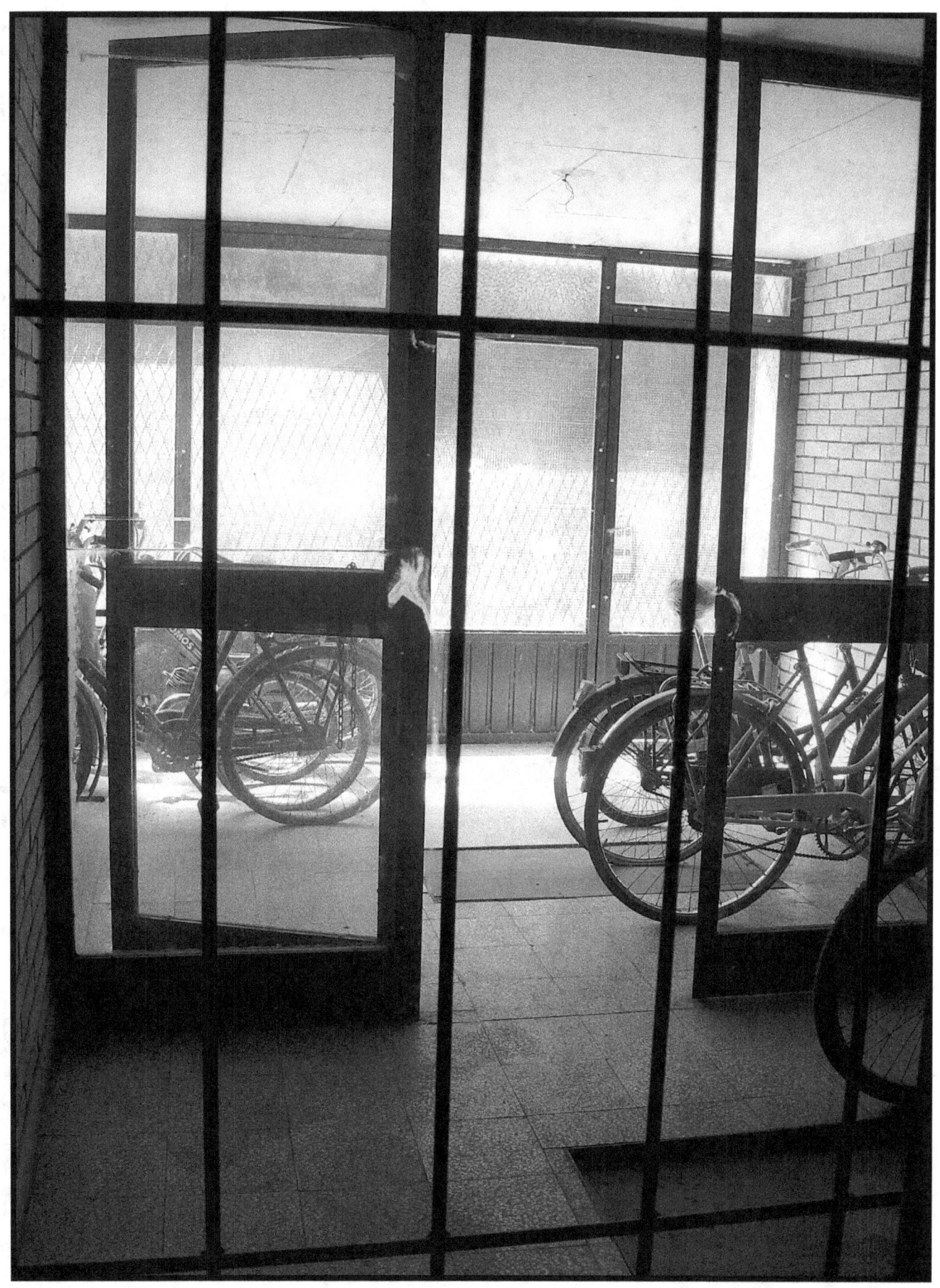

Novi Sad (Serbia) – August 2006

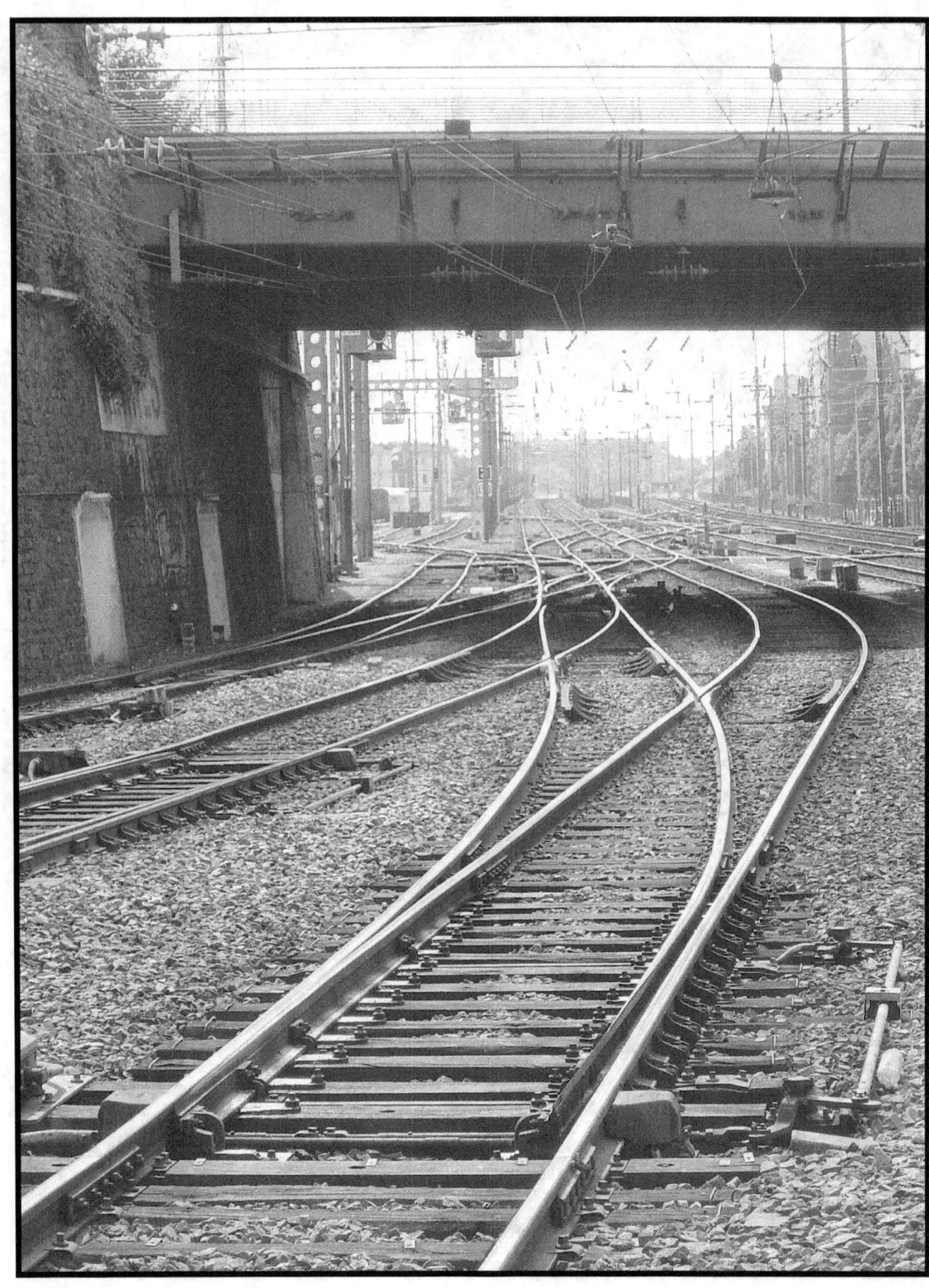

Rennes (France) – July 2006

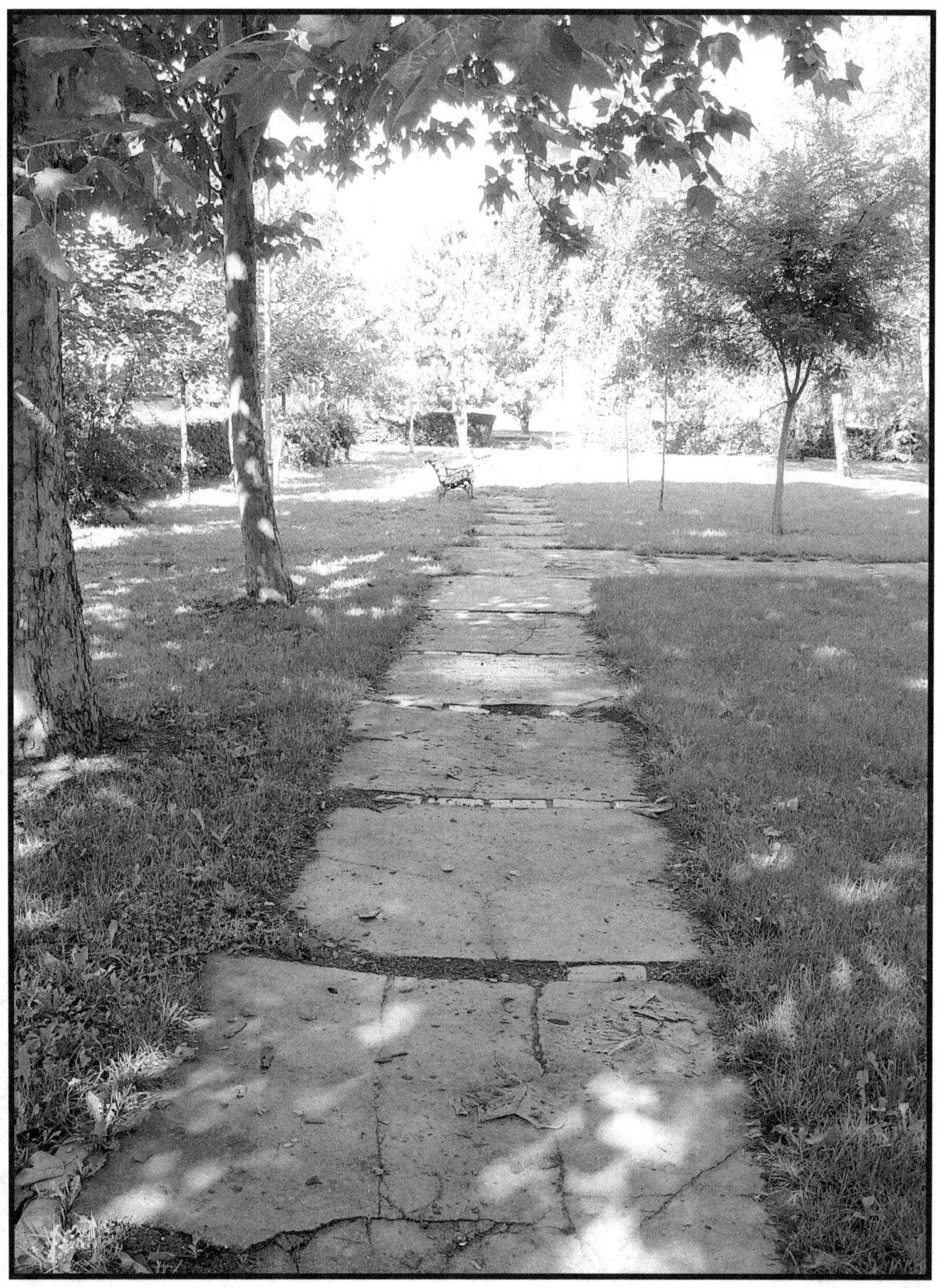

Novi Sad (Serbia) – August 2006

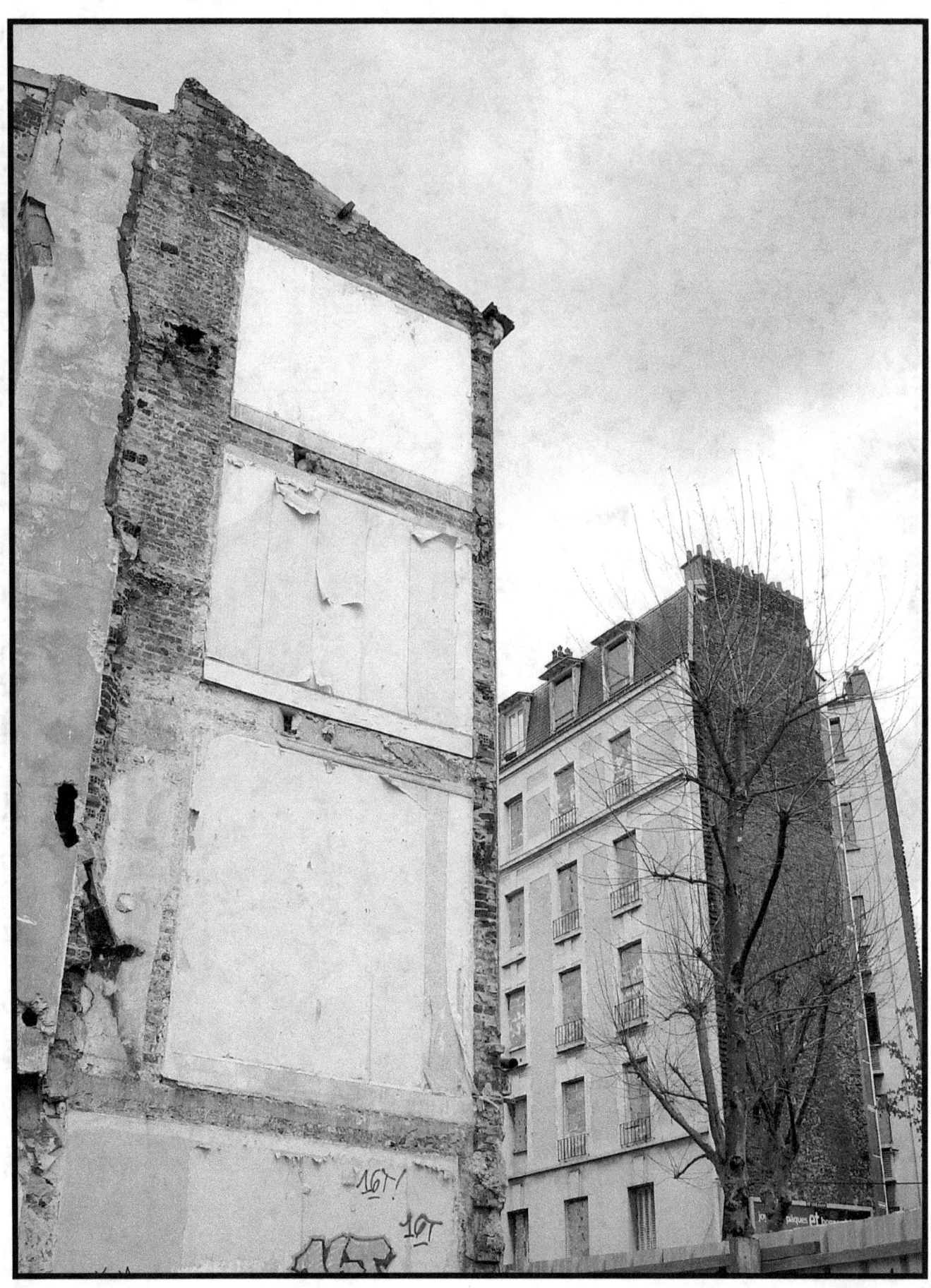

Issy-les-Moulineaux (France) – April 2006

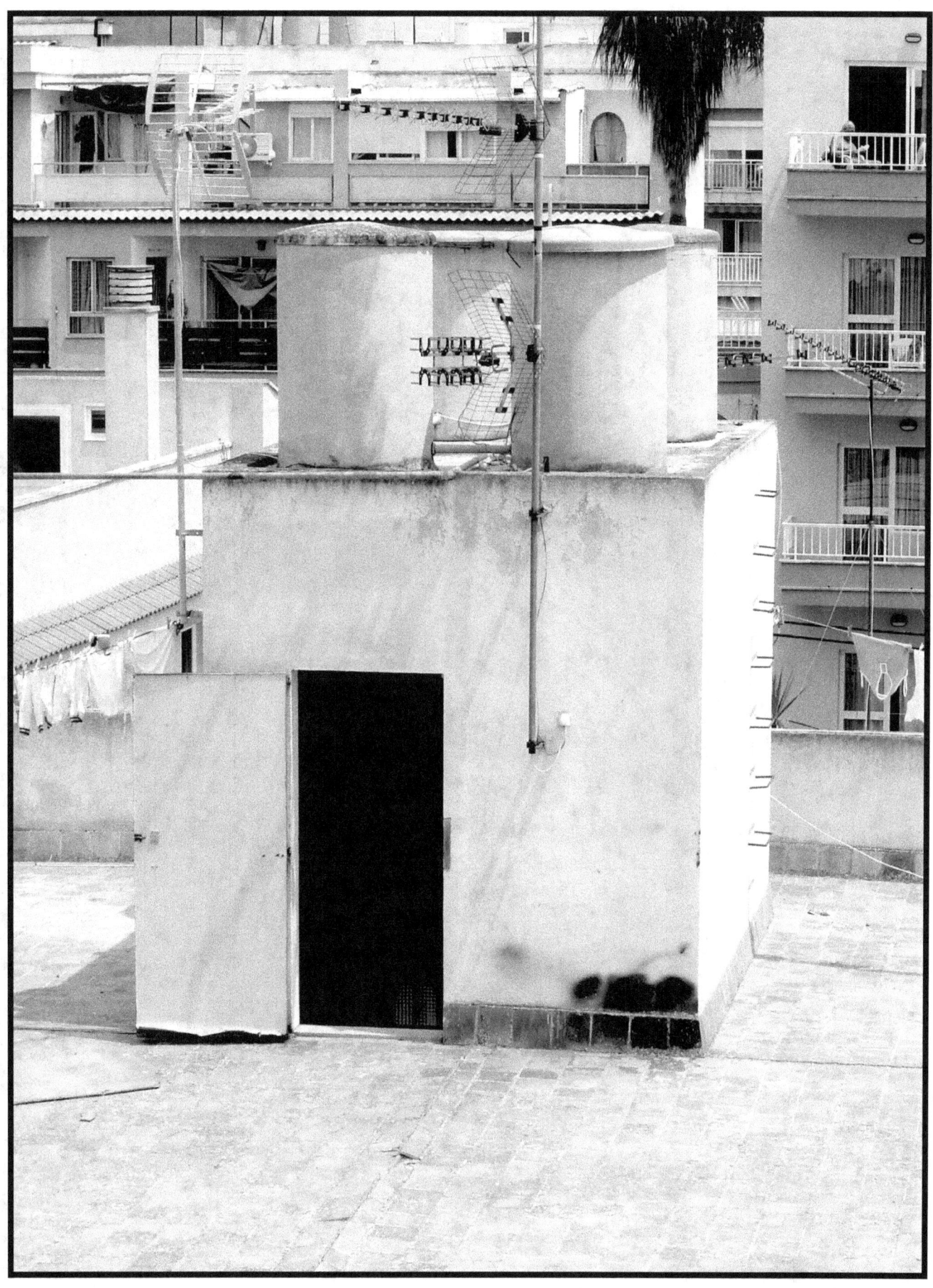

Mallorca (Spain) – June 2005

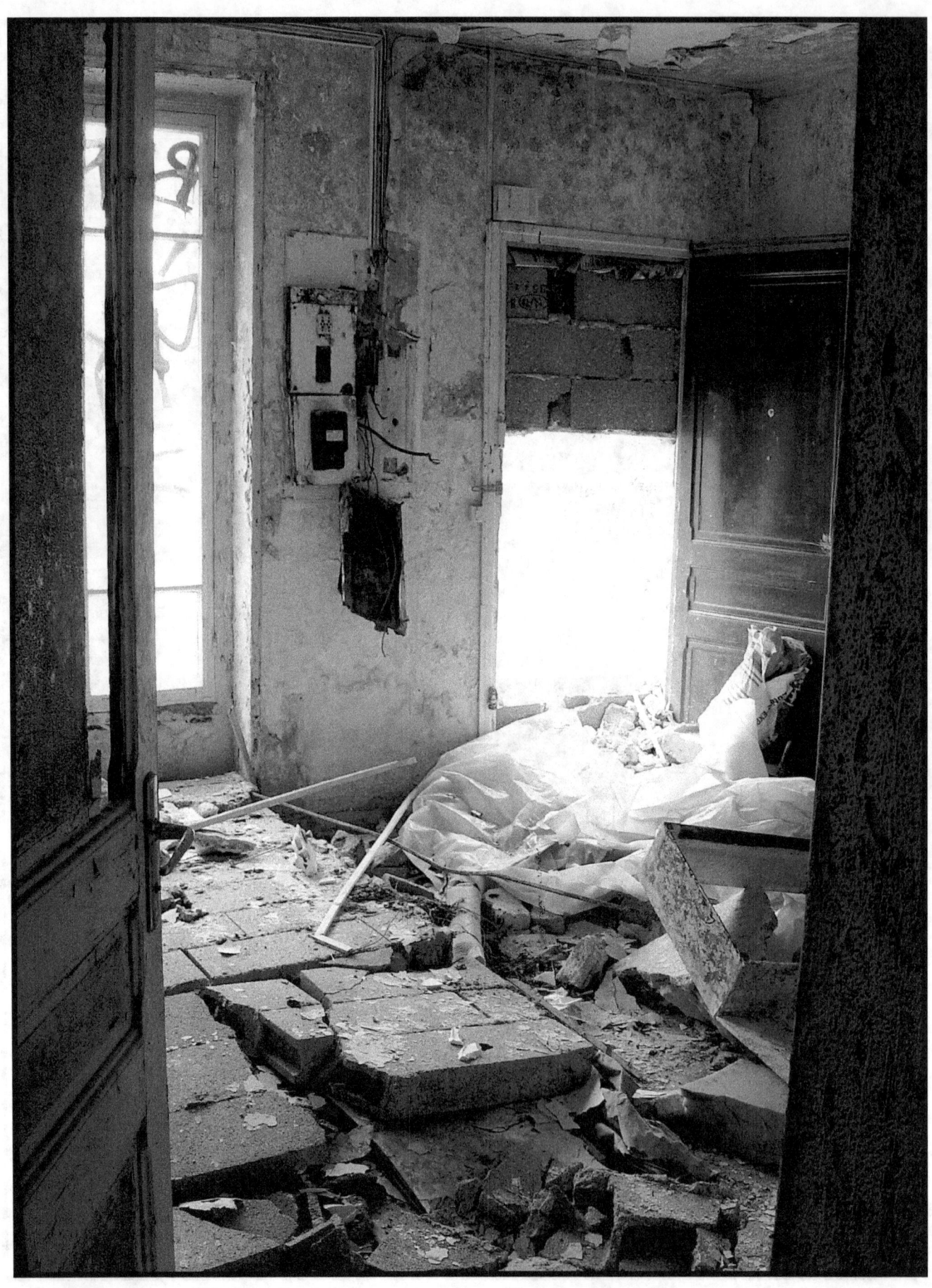

Issy-les-Moulineaux (France) – April 2006

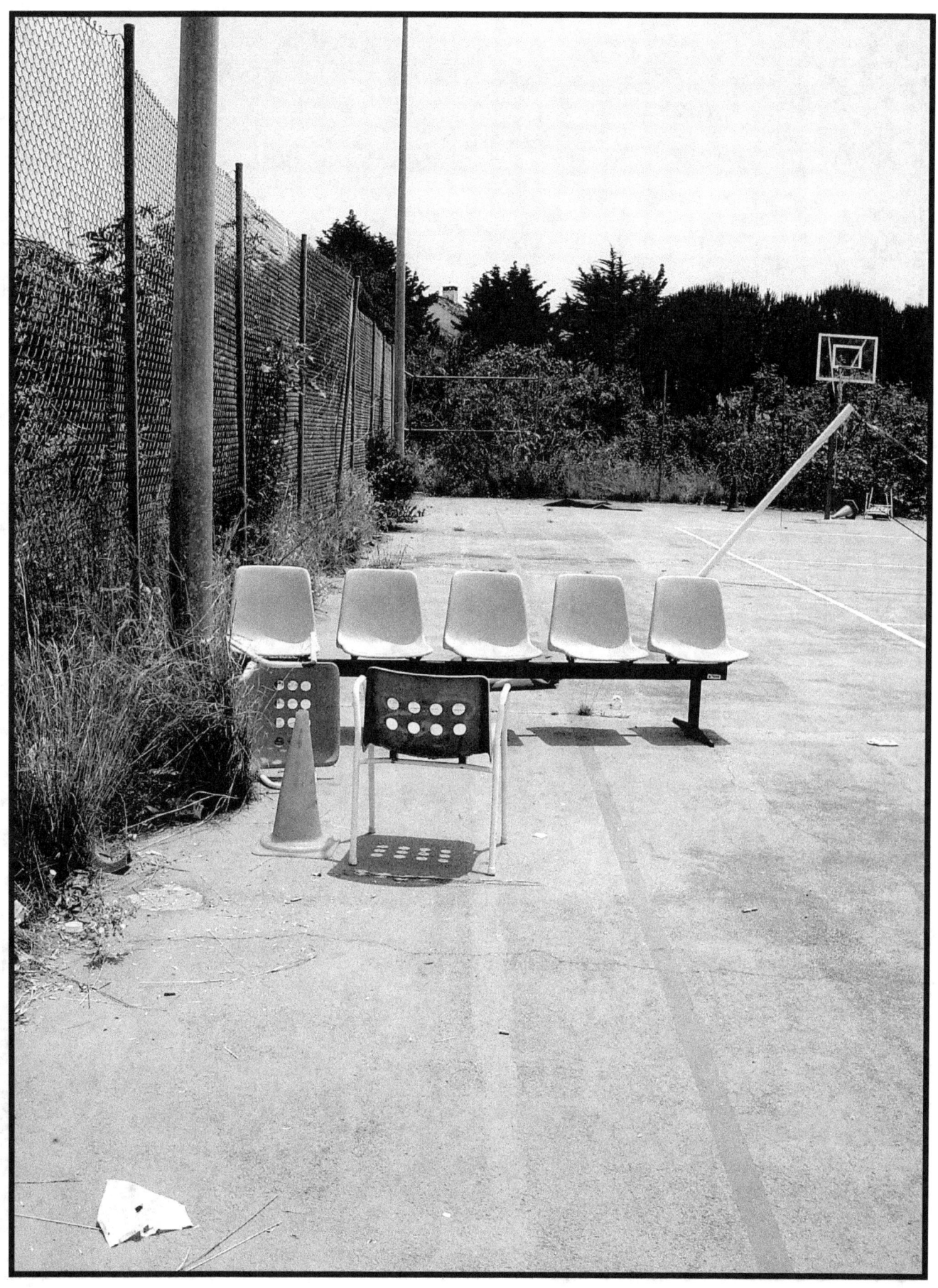

Marbella (Spain) – June 2004

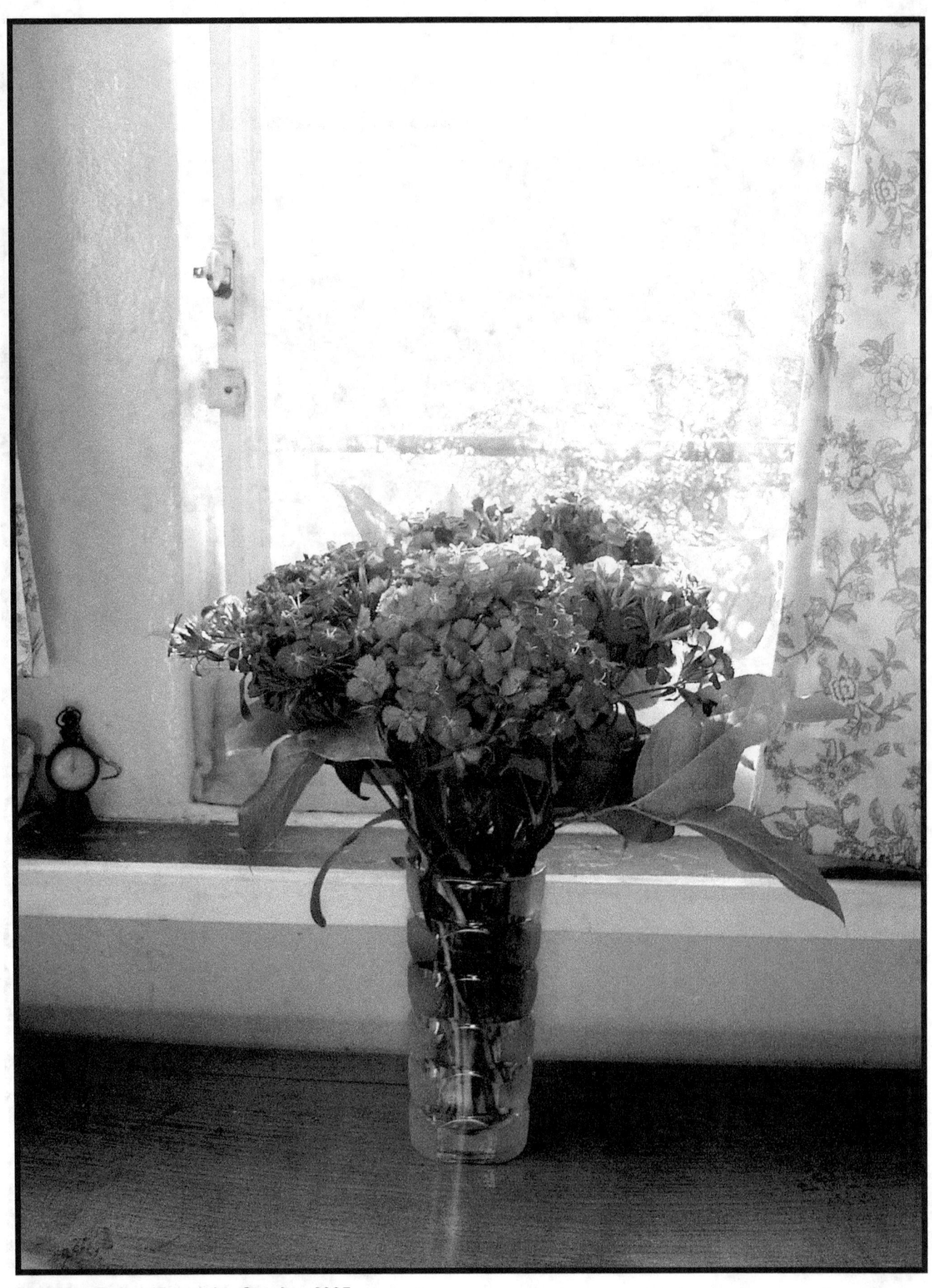

Bourg-la-Reine (France) – October 2005

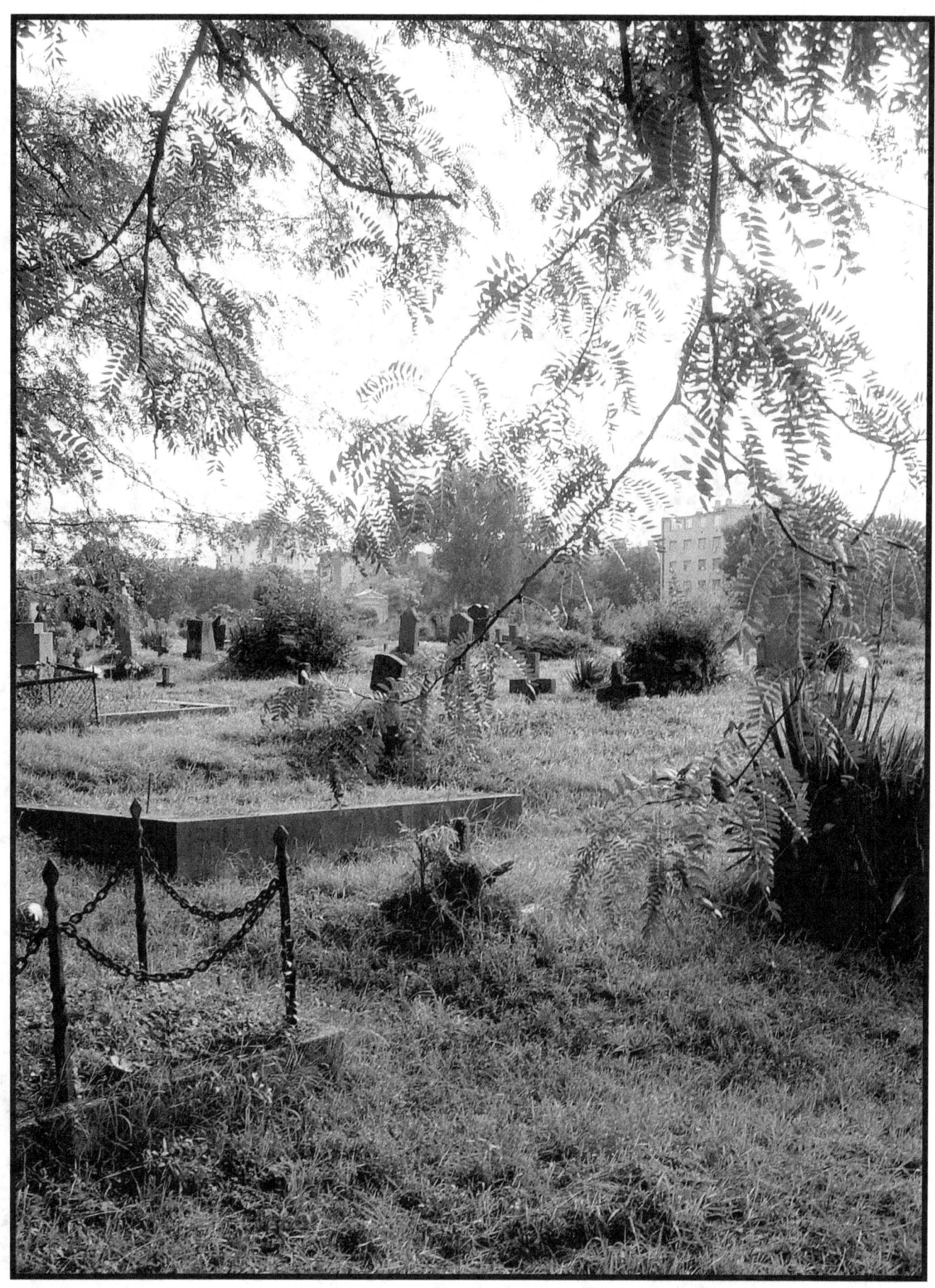

Novi Sad (Serbia) – August 2006

Paris (France) – April 2004

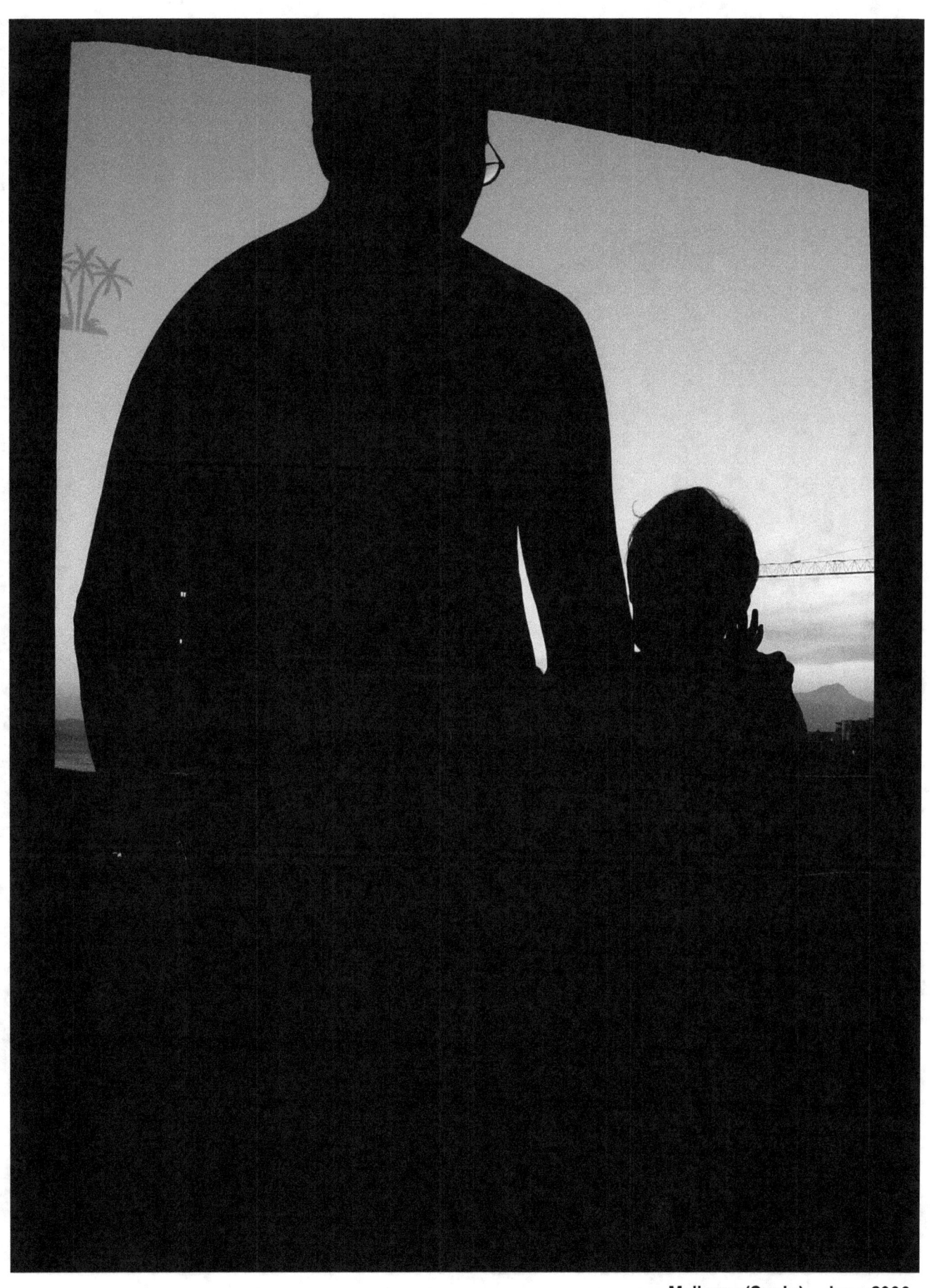

Mallorca (Spain) – June 2006

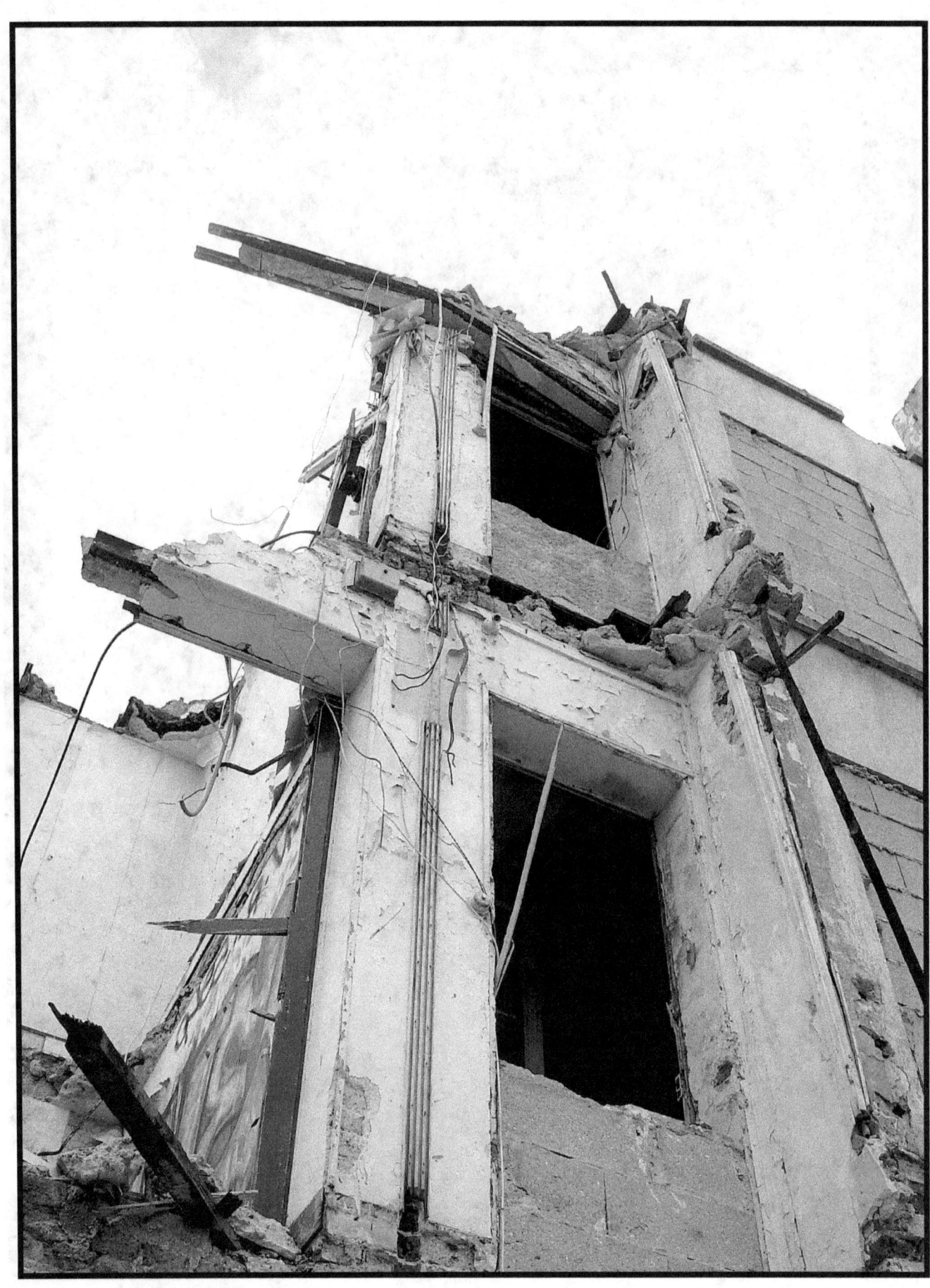

Issy-les-Moulineaux (France) – April 2006

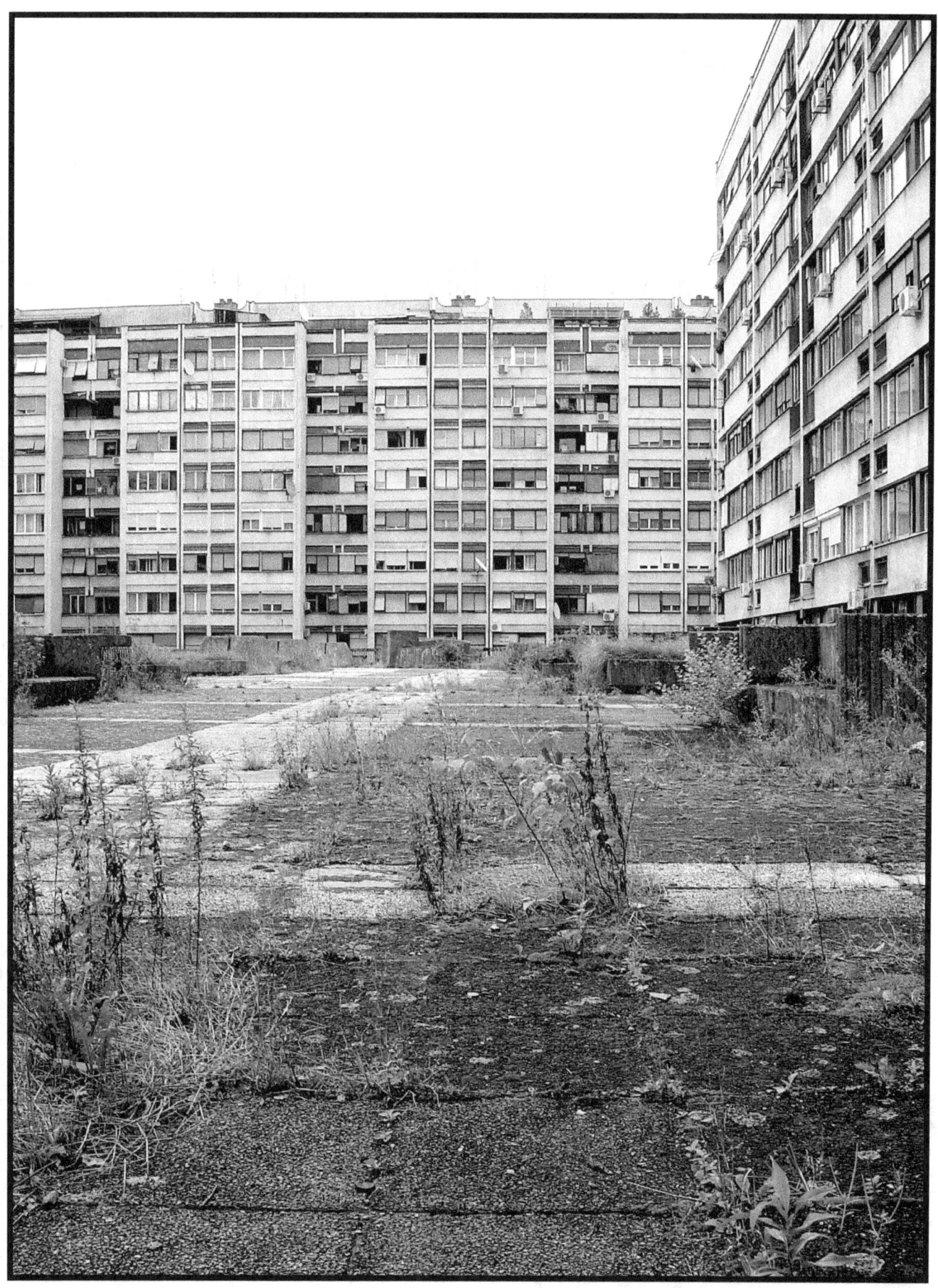

Novi Sad (Serbia) – August 2006

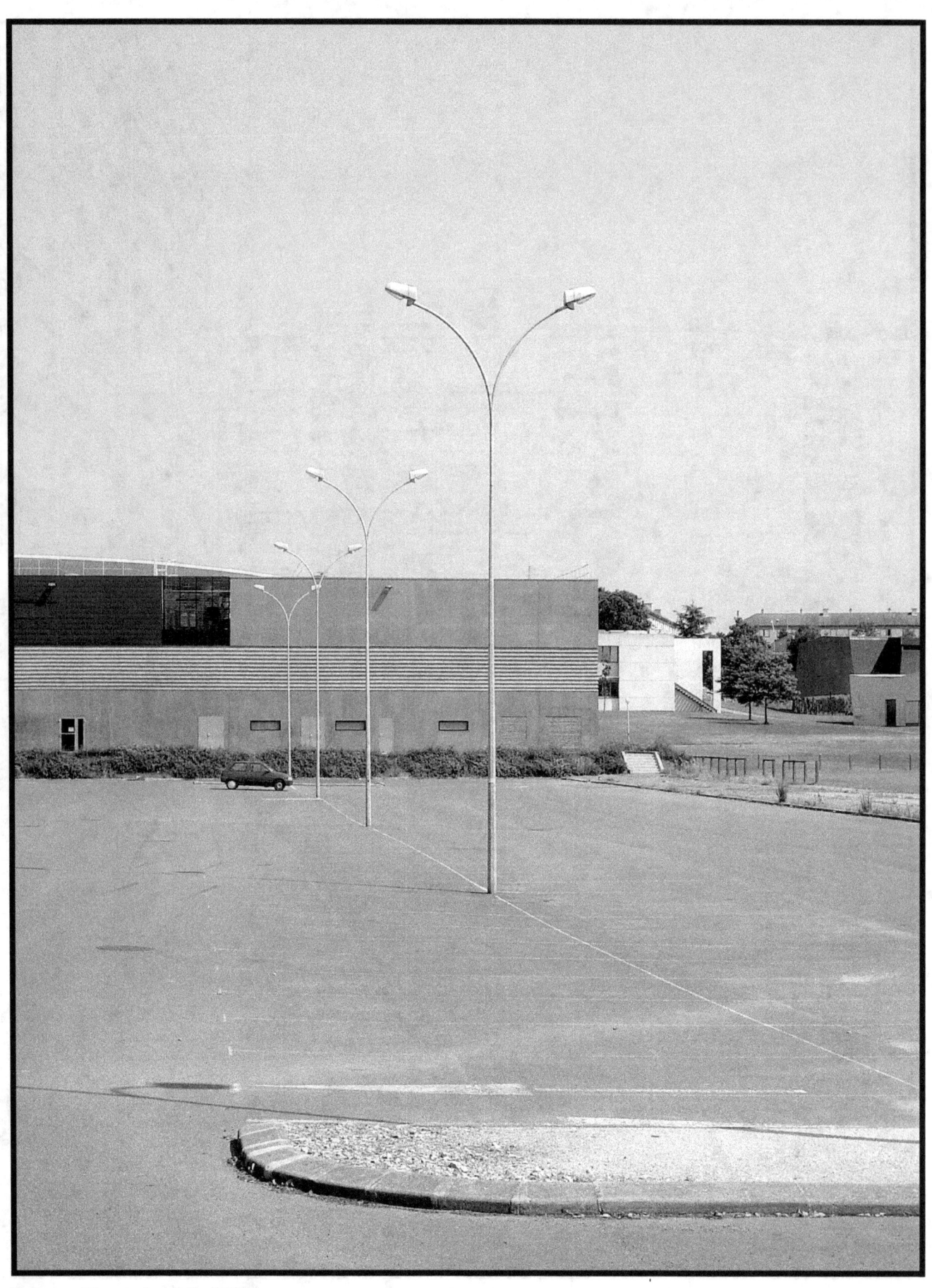

Rennes (France) – July 2006

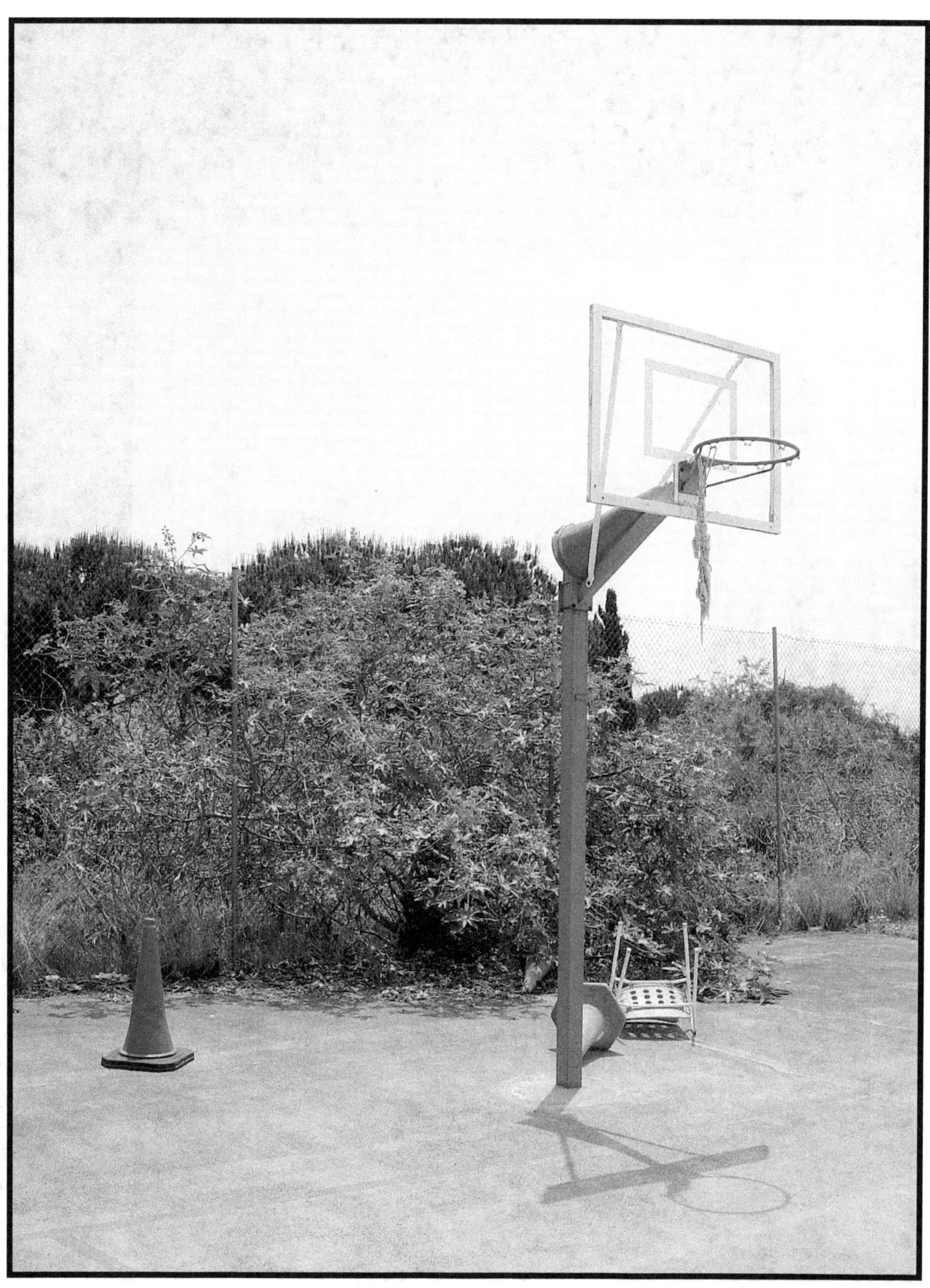

Marbella (Spain) – June 2004

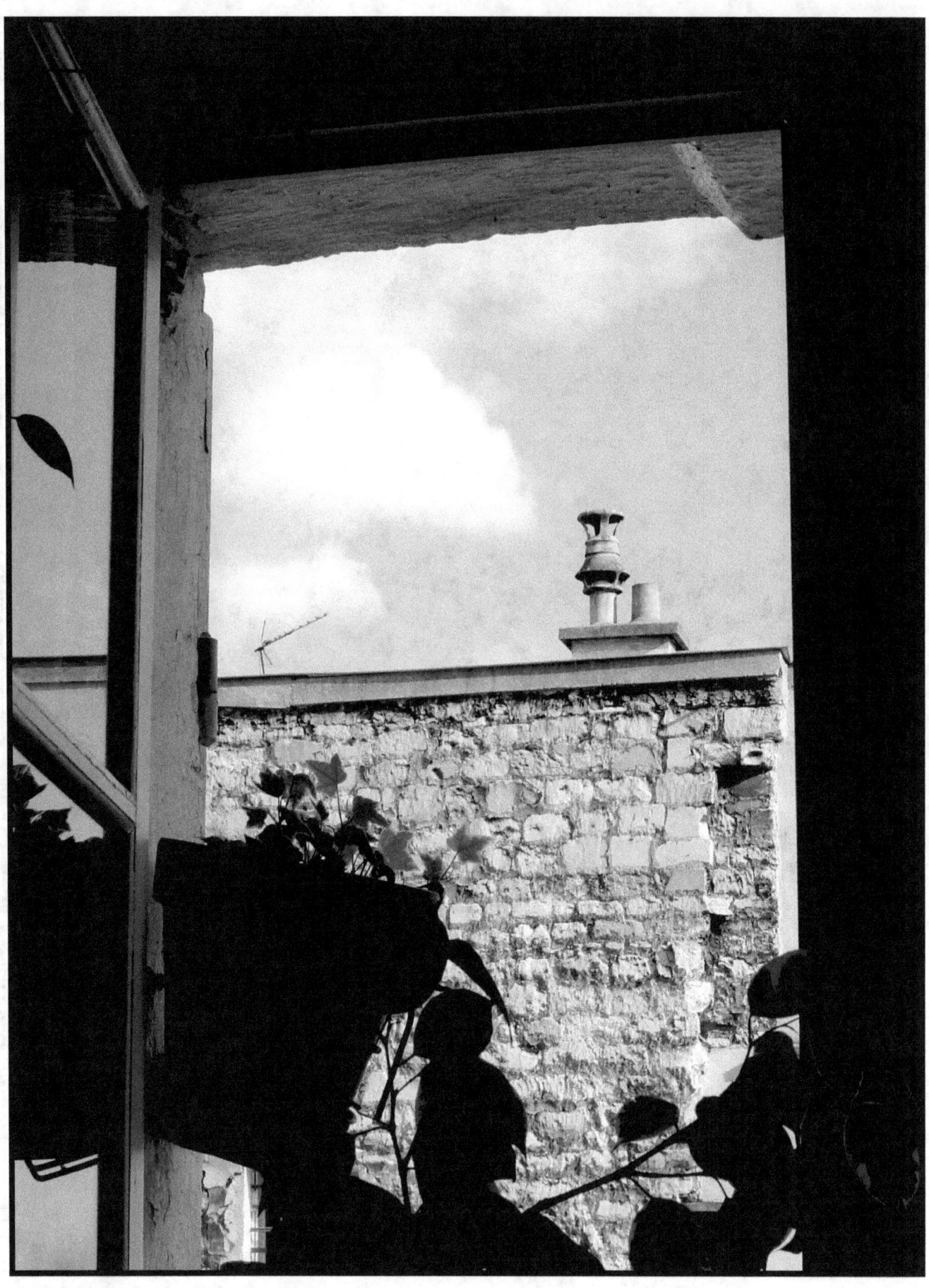

Paris (France) – April 2004

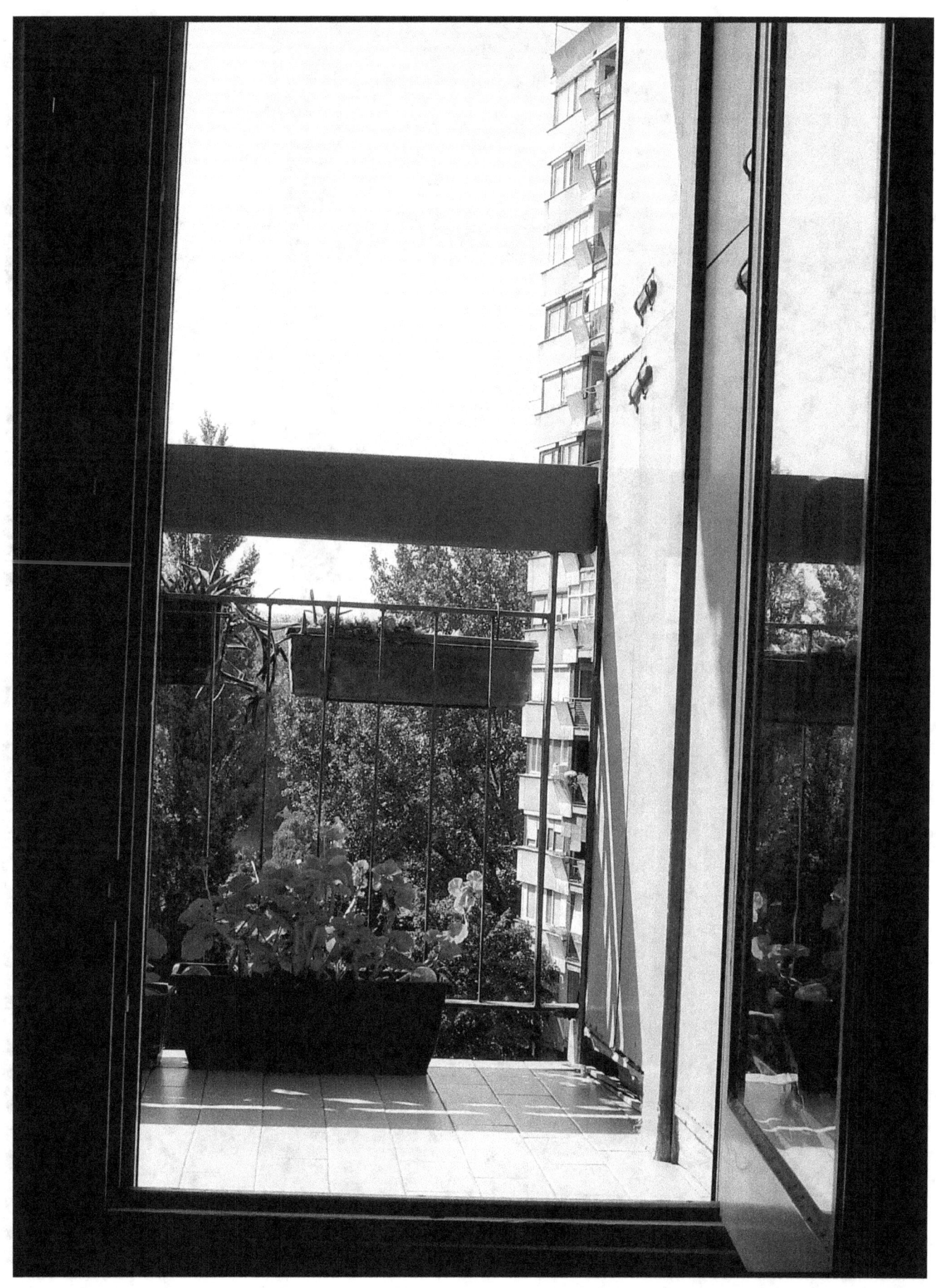

Novi Sad (Serbia) – August 2006

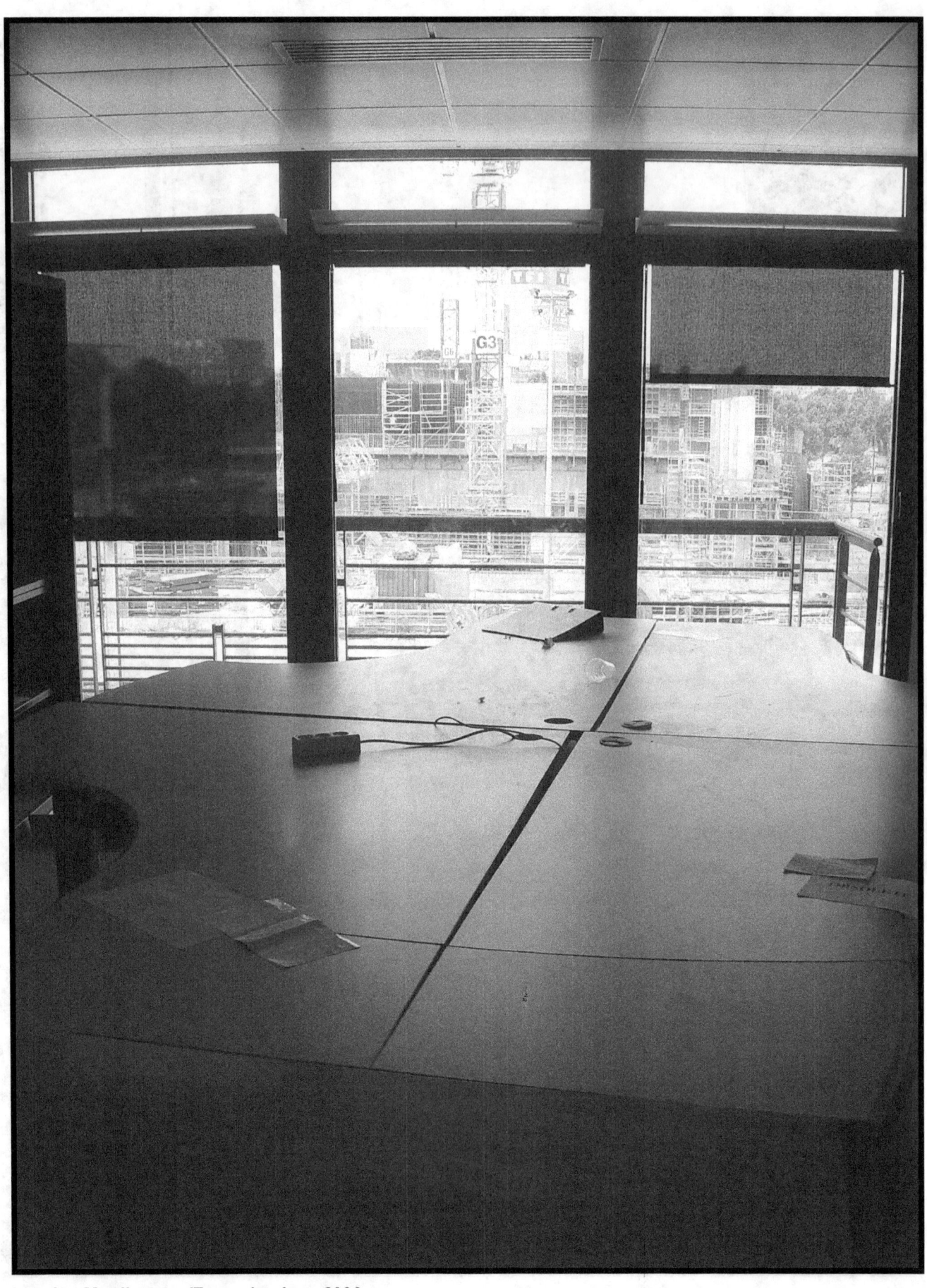

Issy-les-Moulineaux (France) – June 2006

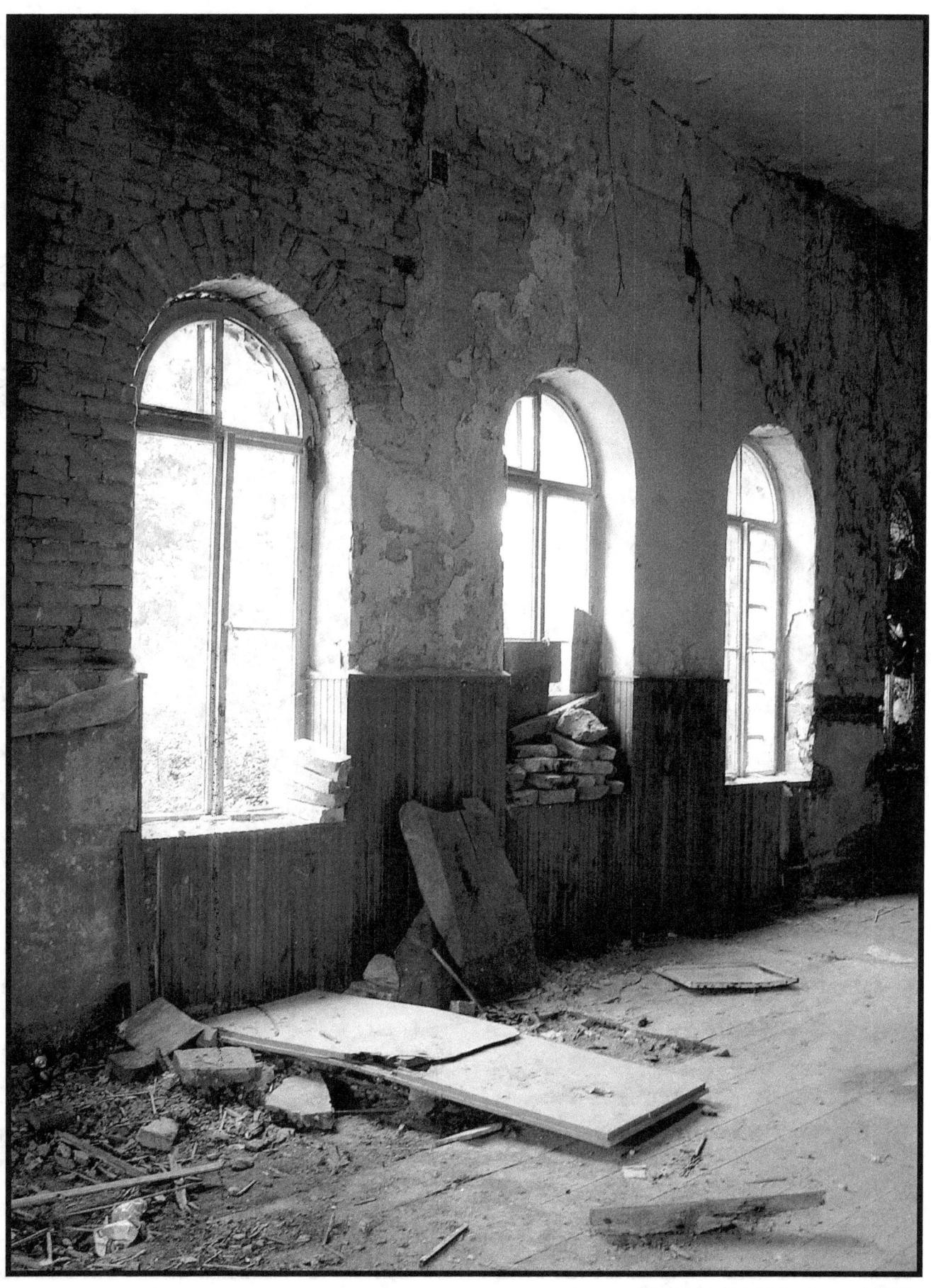

Novi Sad (Serbia) – August 2006

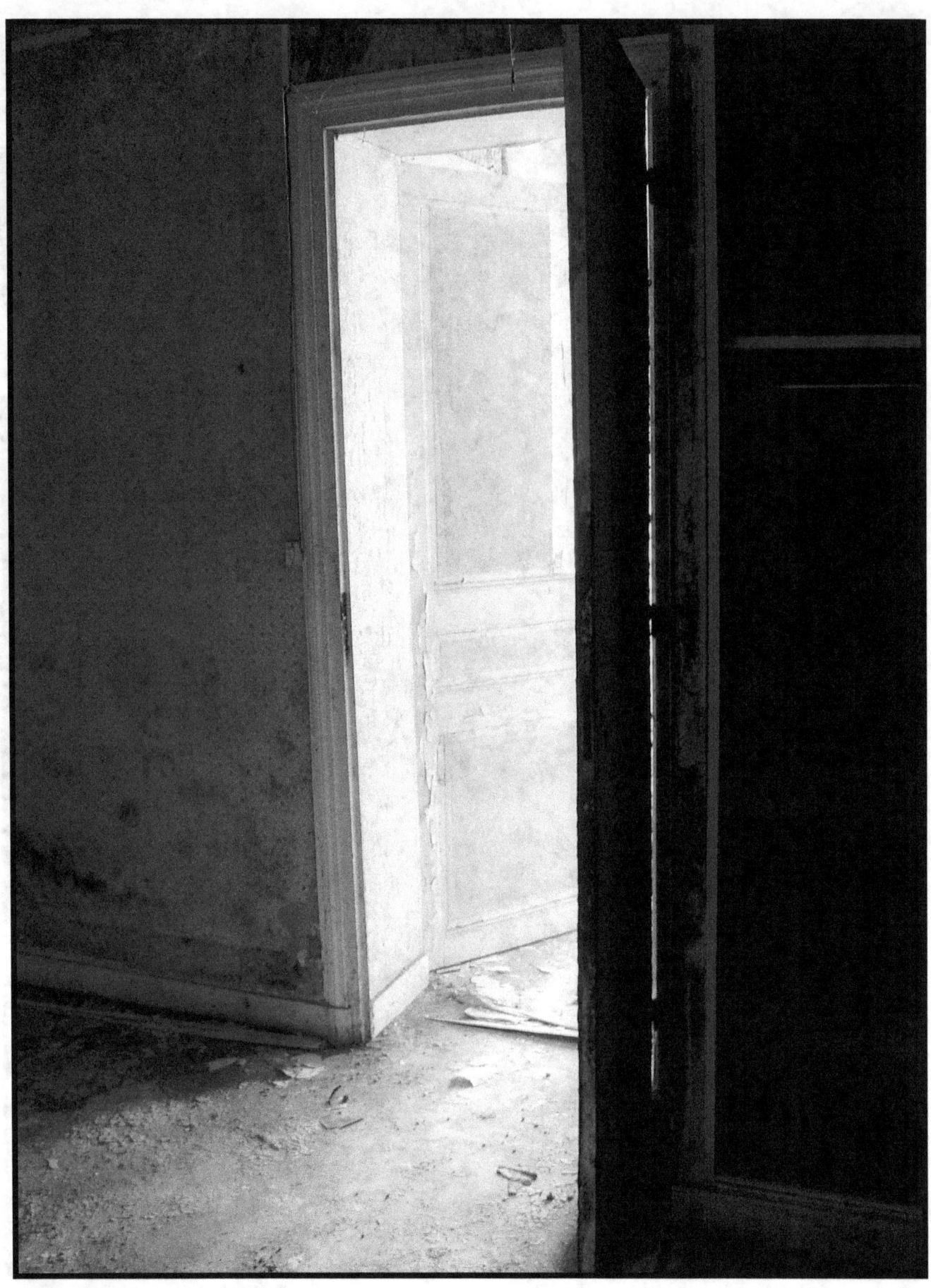

Issy-les-Moulineaux (France) – April 2006

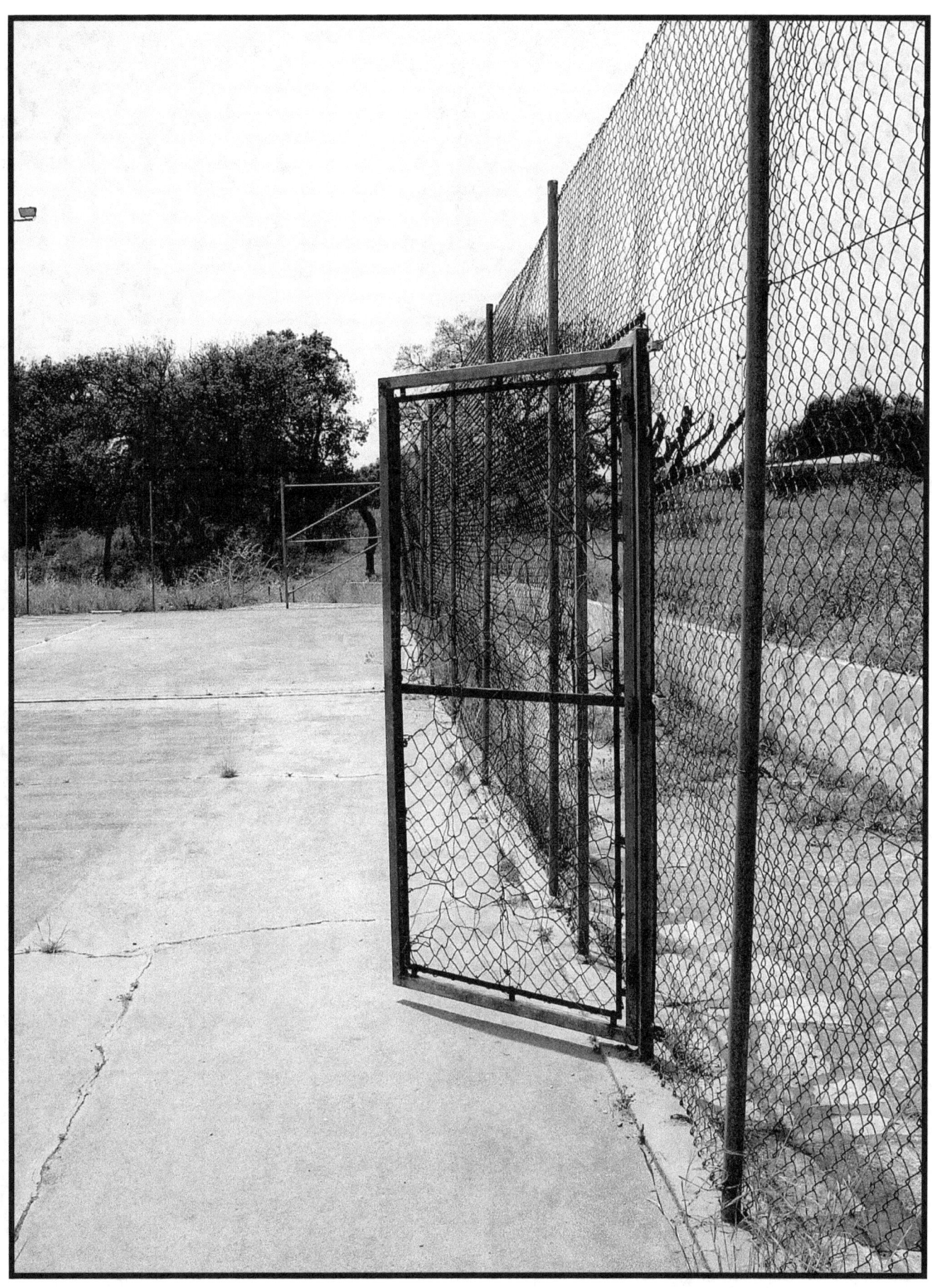

Marbella (Spain) – June 2004

Rennes (France) – November 2004

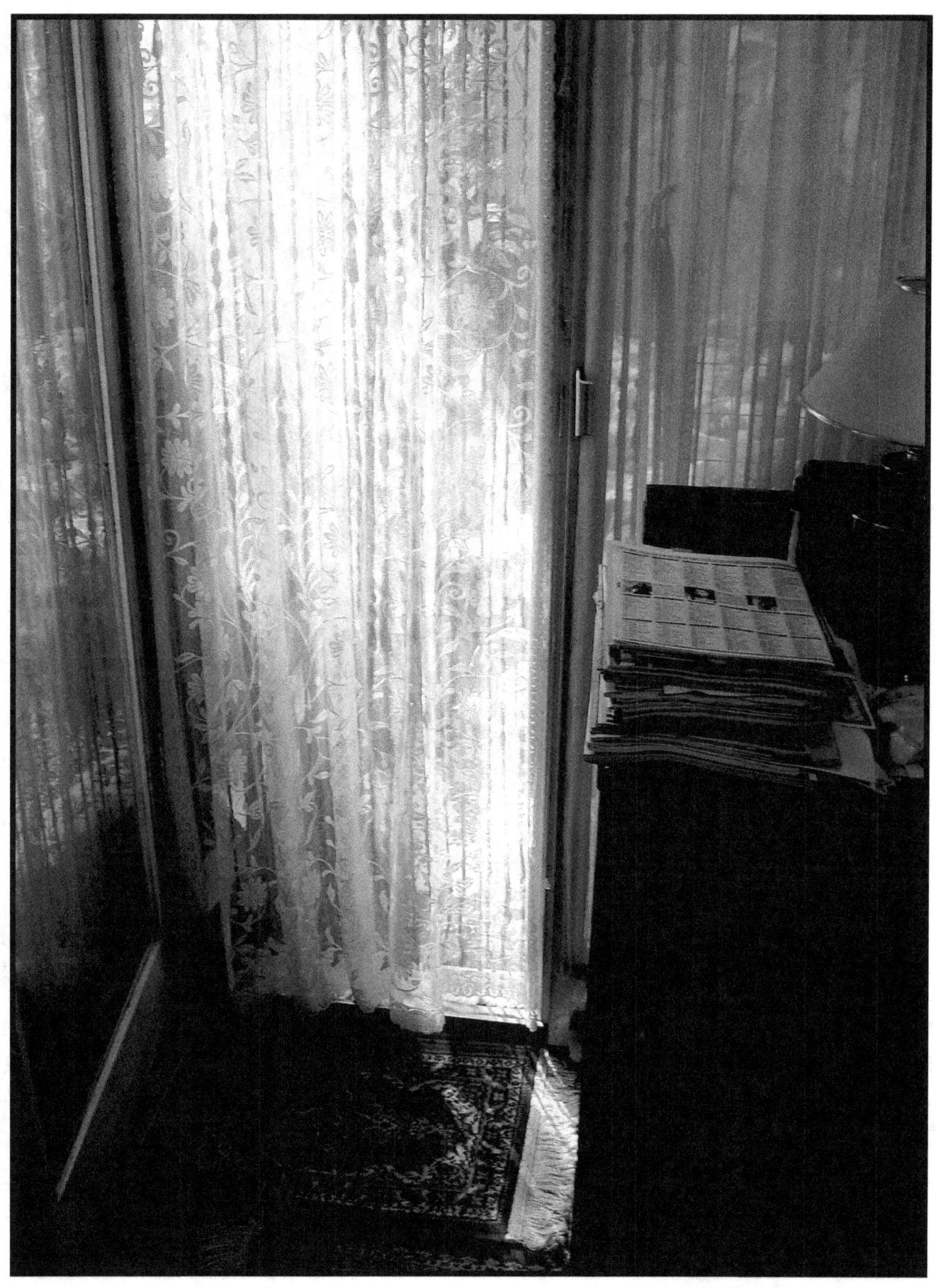

Novi Sad (Serbia) – August 2006

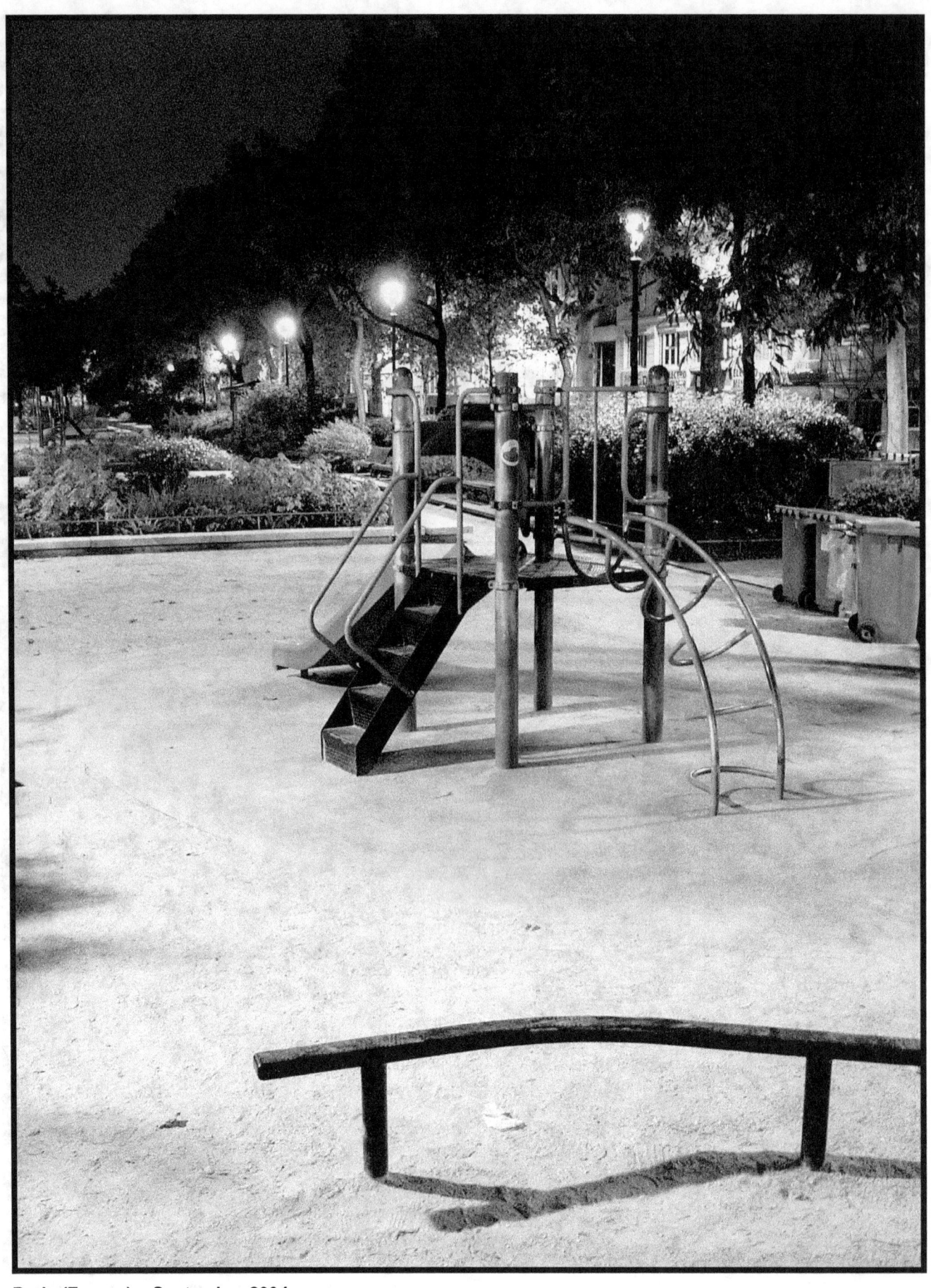

Paris (France) – September 2004

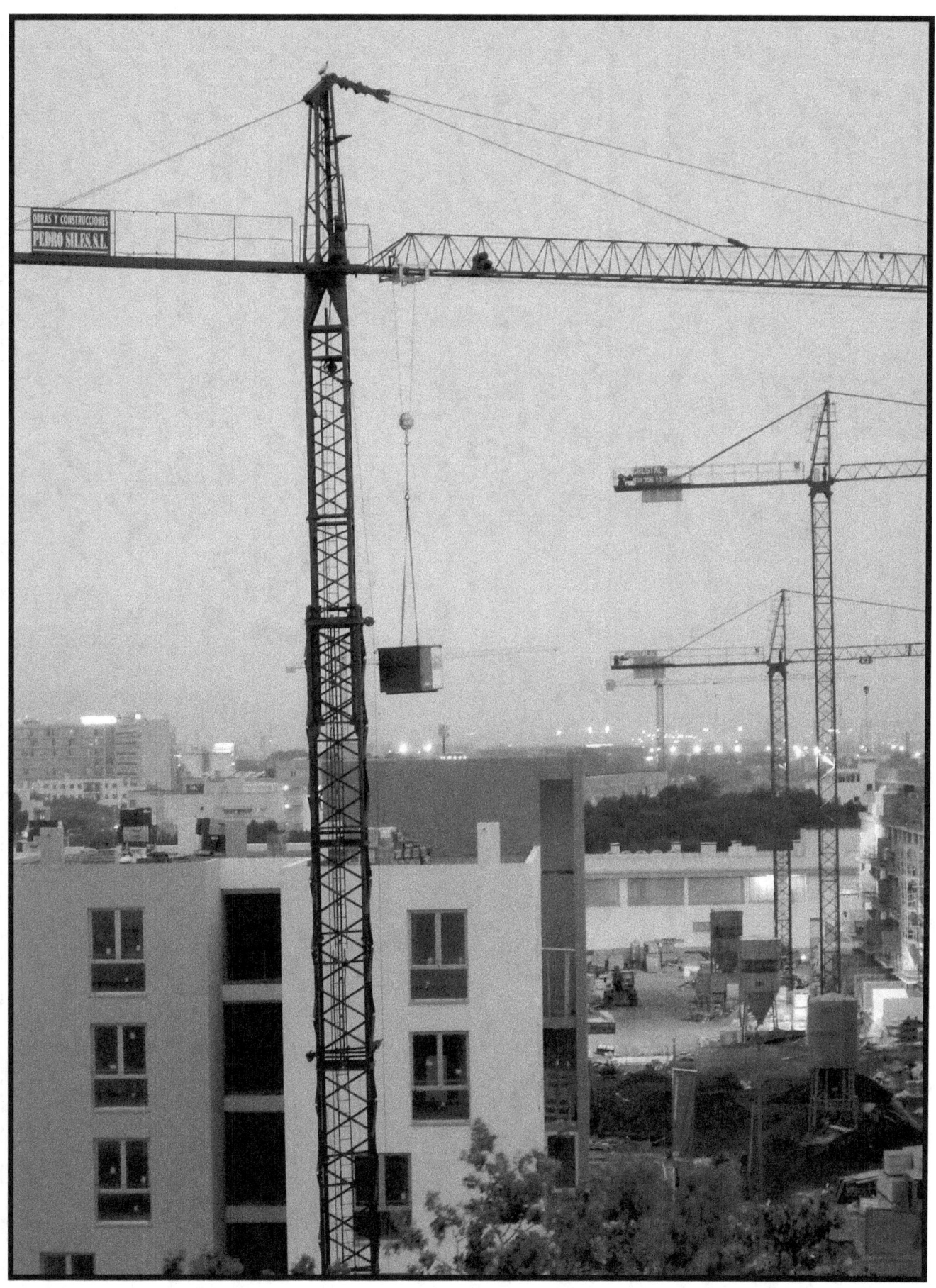

Mallorca (Spain) – June 2006

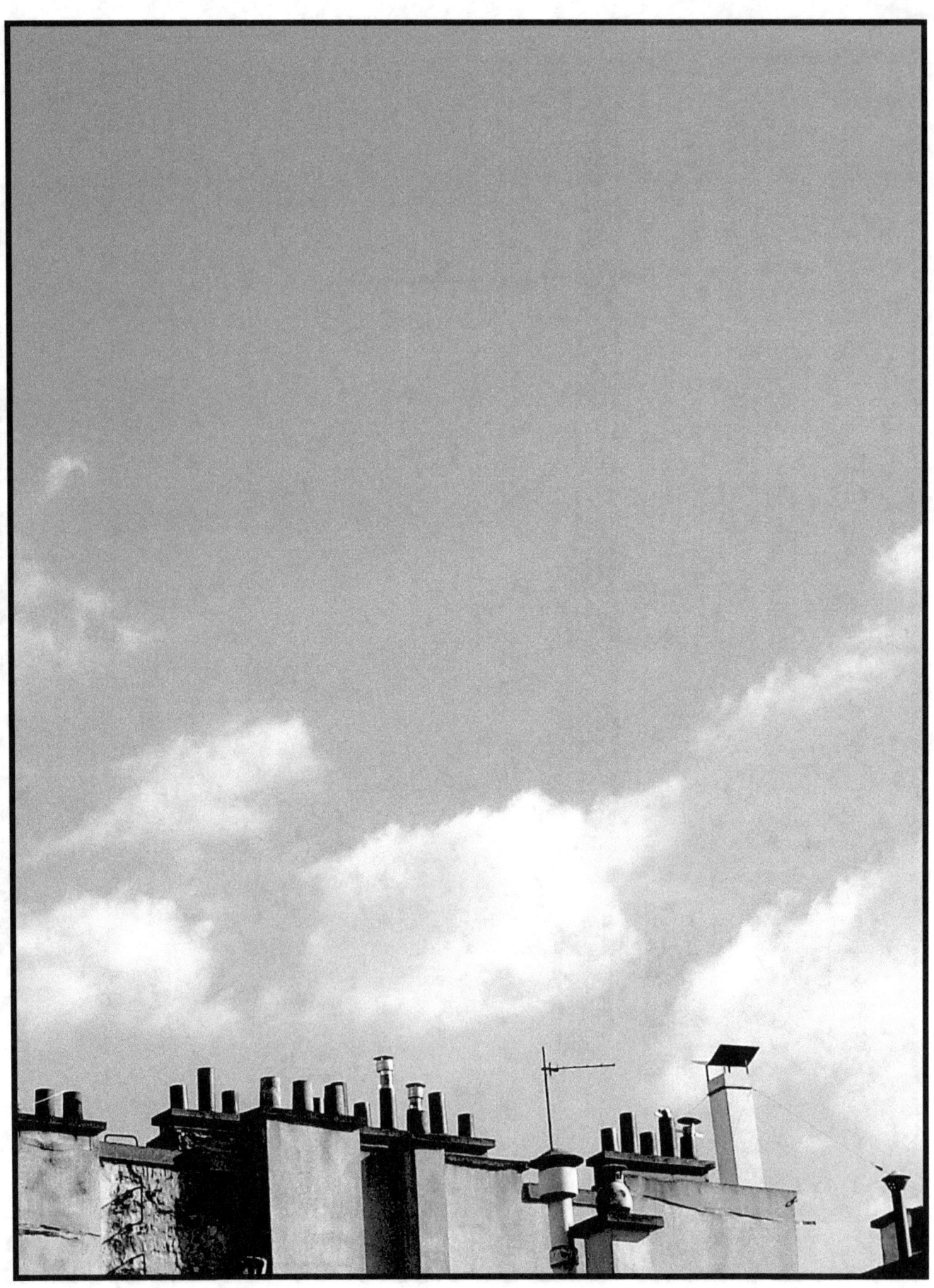

Paris (France) – April 2004

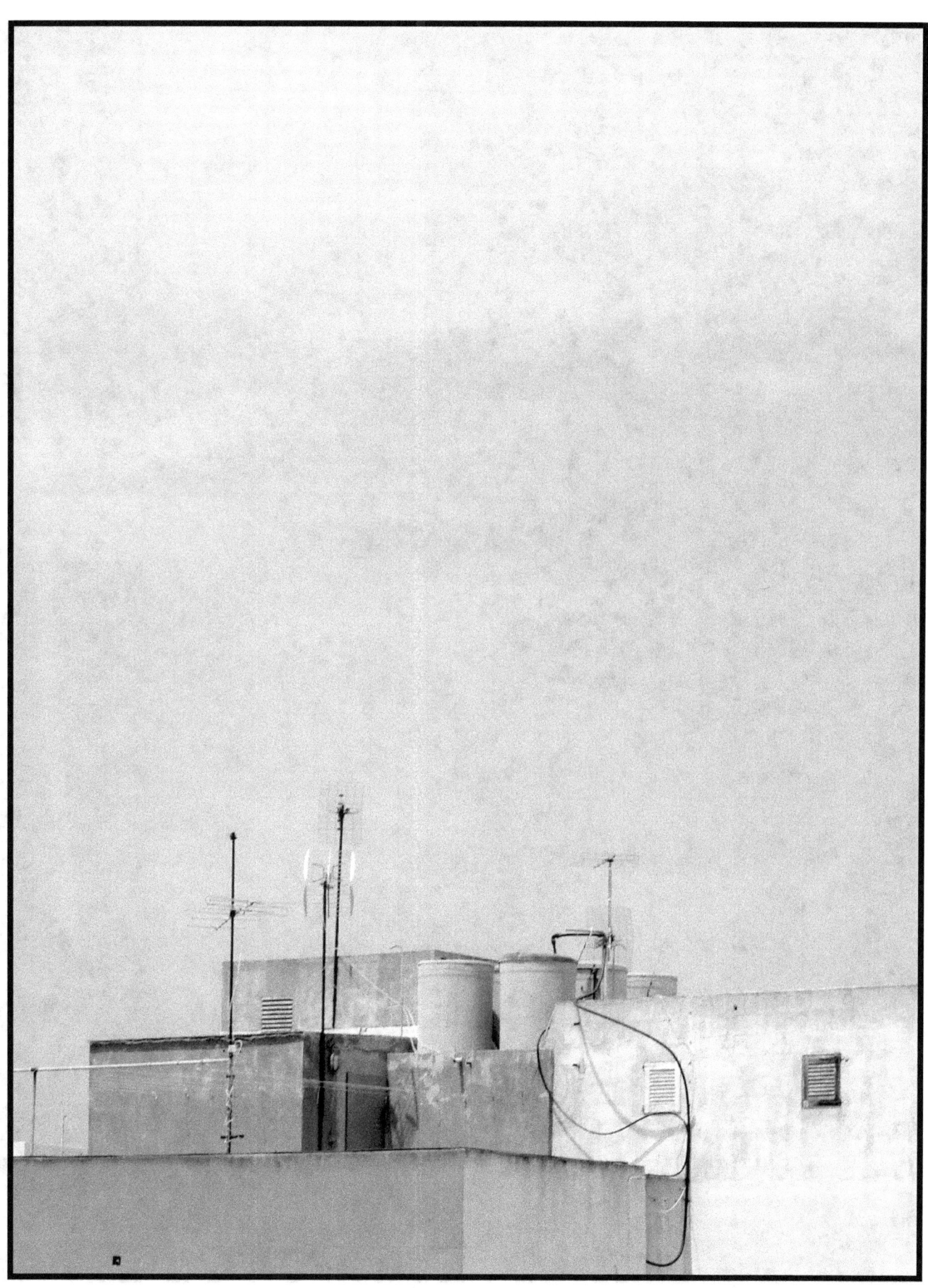

Mallorca (Spain) – June 2005

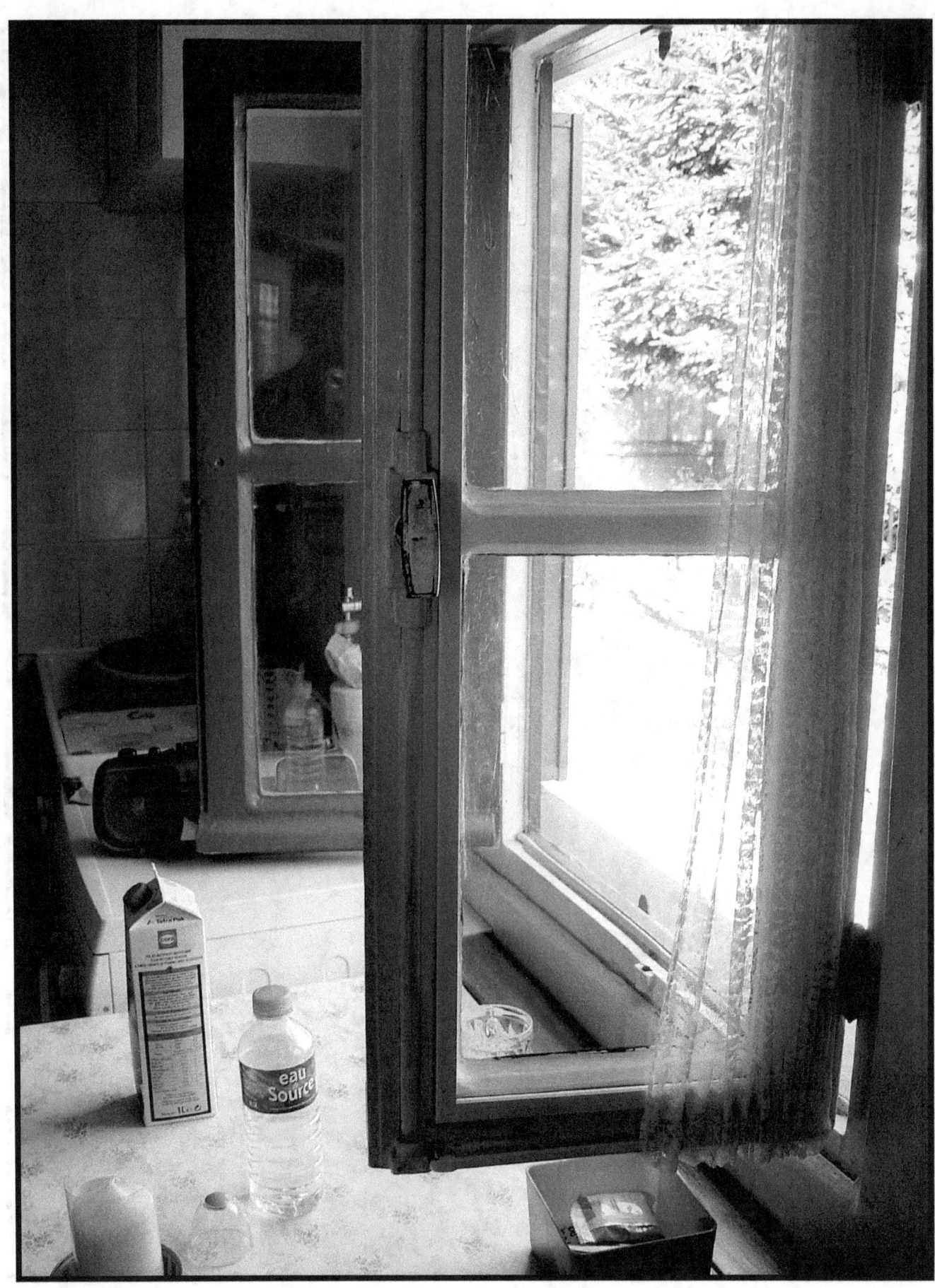

Bourg-la-Reine (France) – October 2005

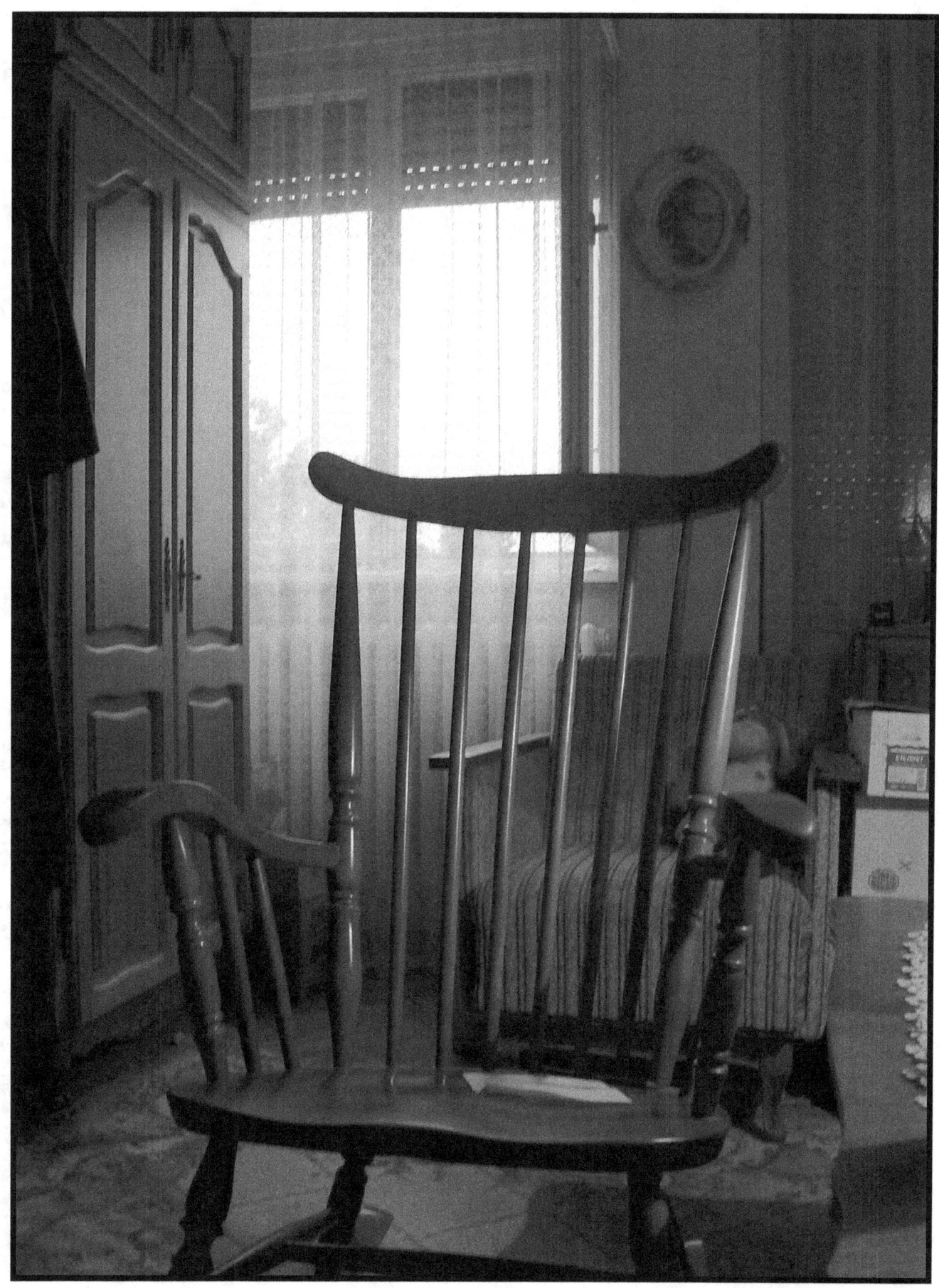

Novi Sad (Serbia) – August 2006

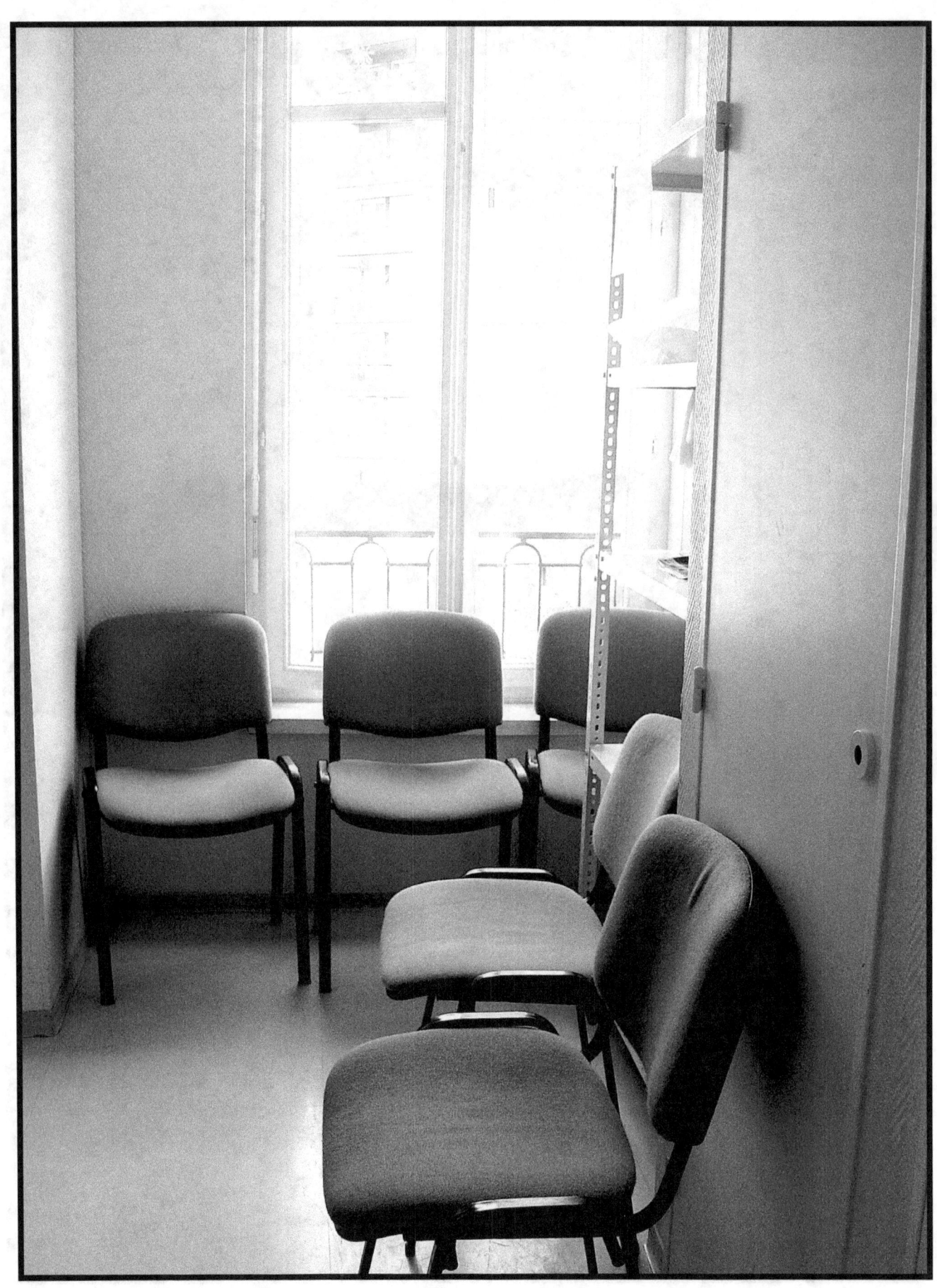

Paris (France) – September 2004

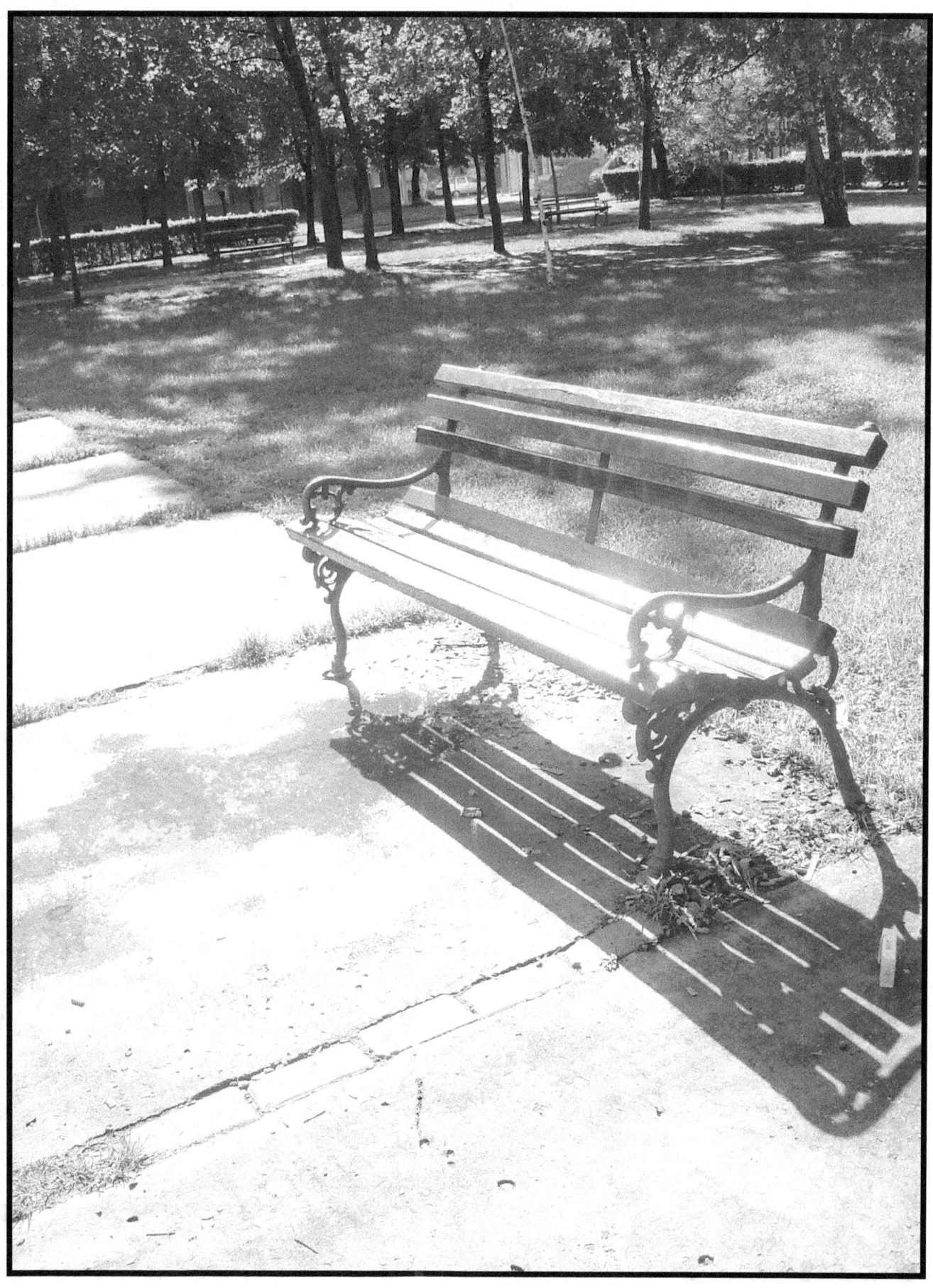

Novi Sad (Serbia) – August 2006

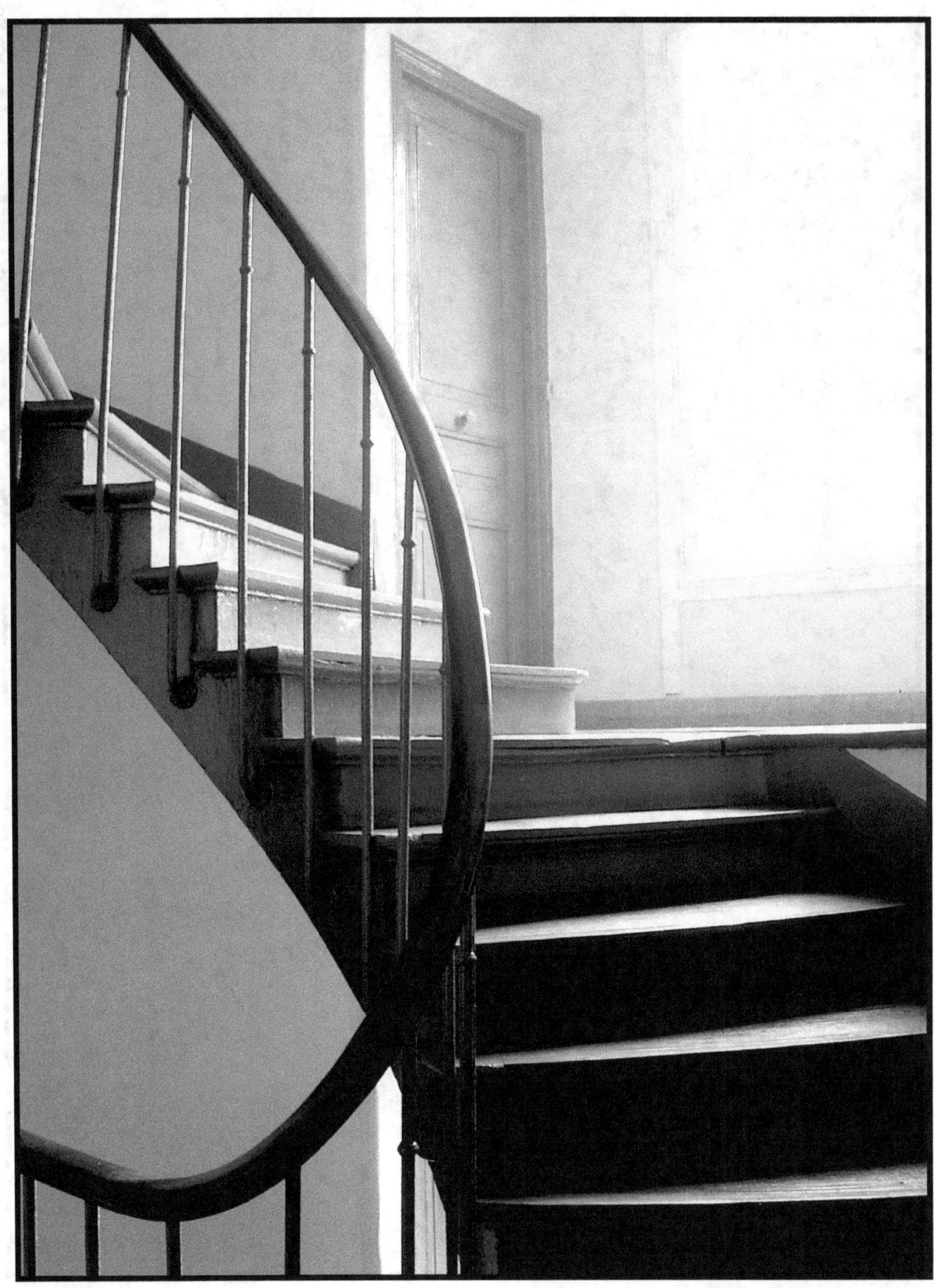

Paris (France) – January 2006

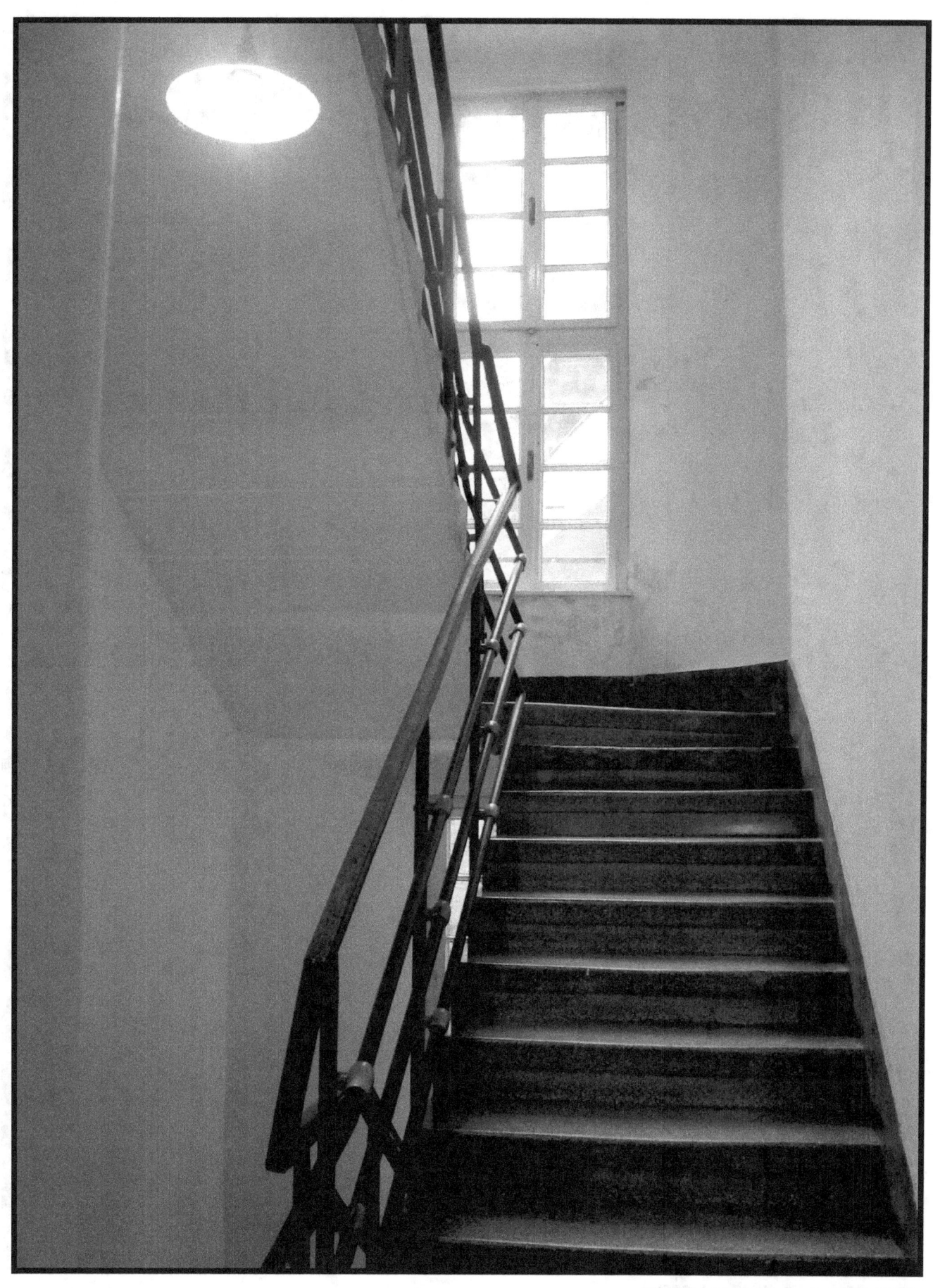

Novi Sad (Serbia) – August 2006

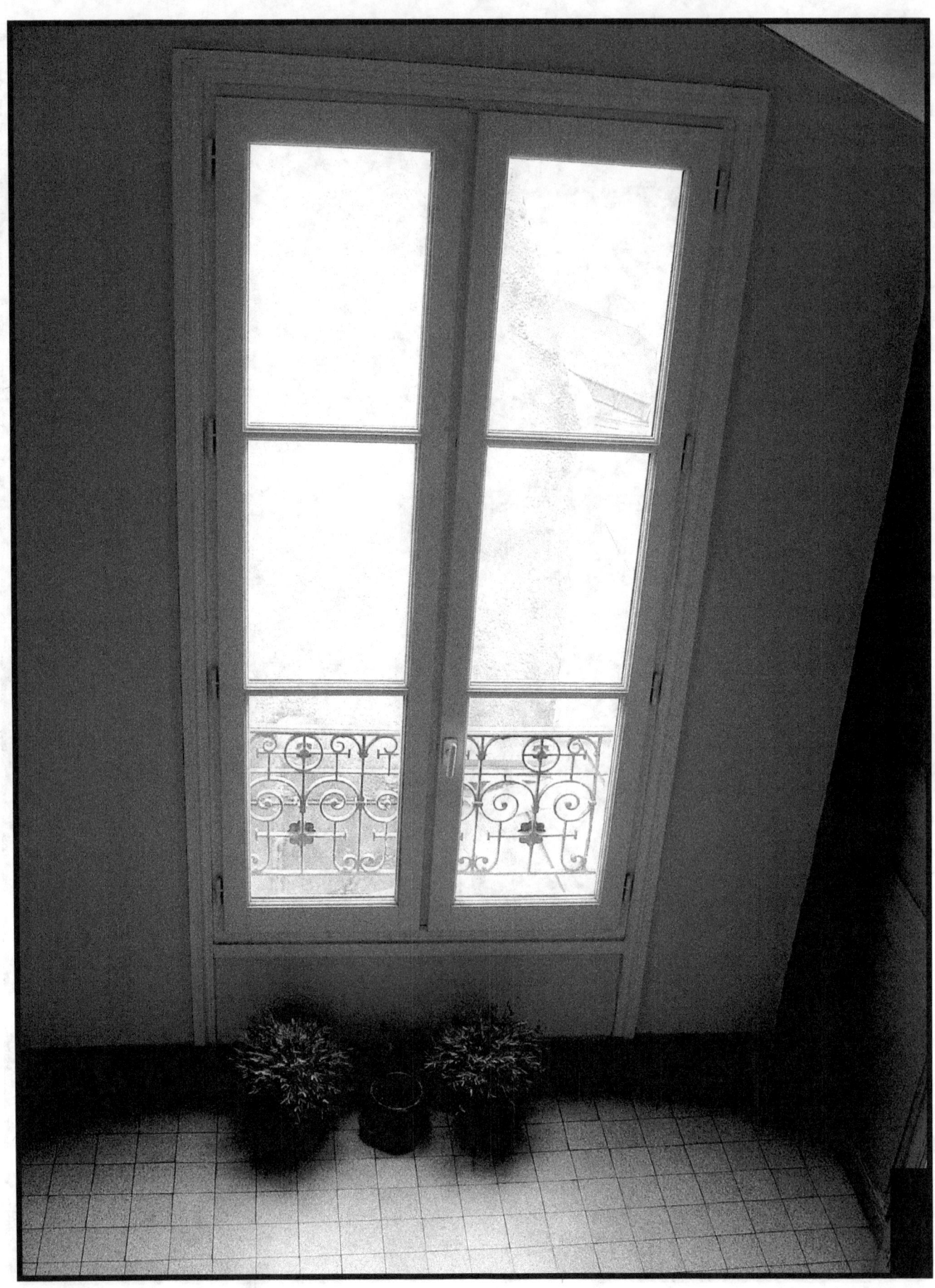

Paris (France) – January 2006

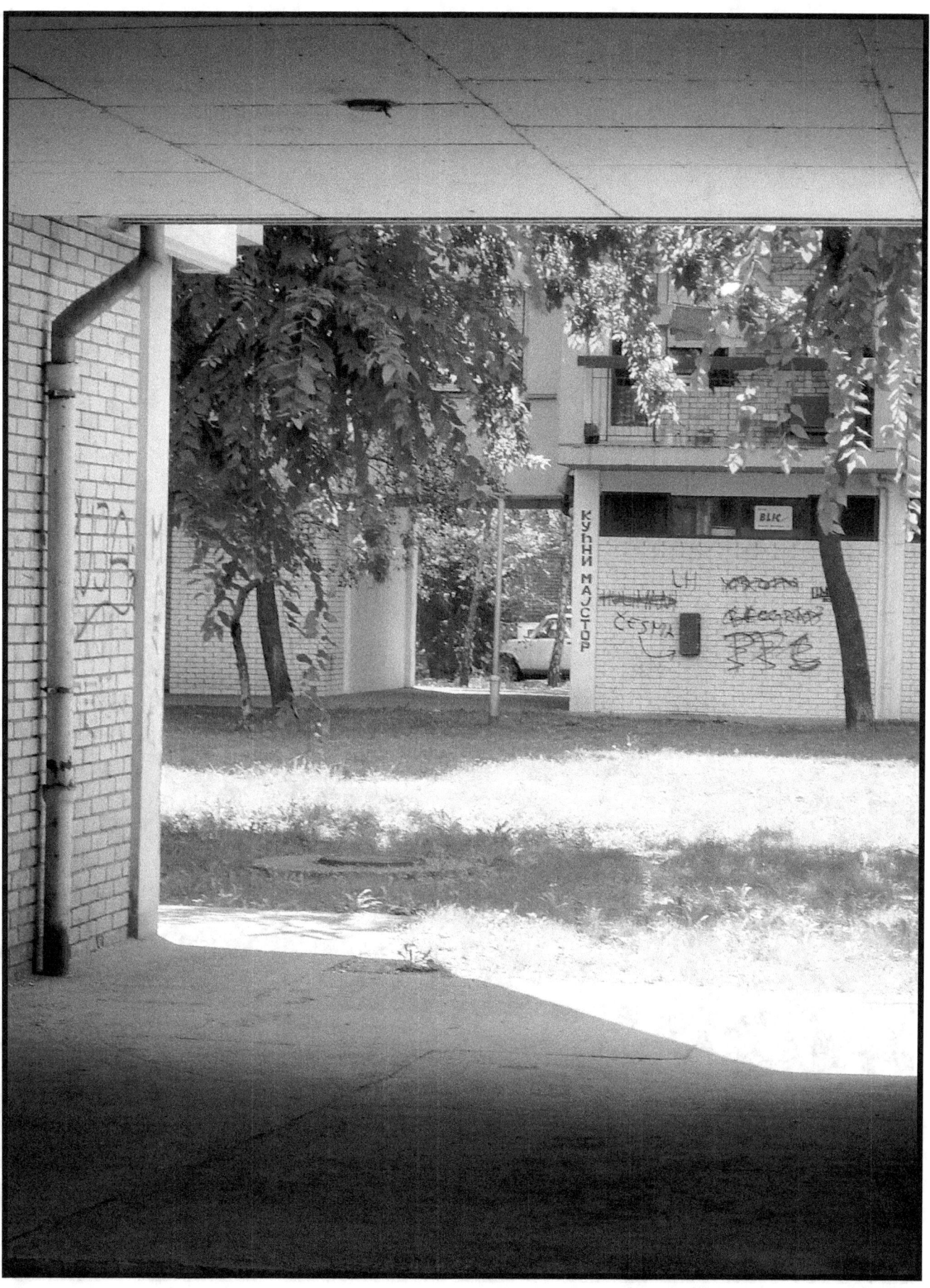

Novi Sad (Serbia) – August 2006

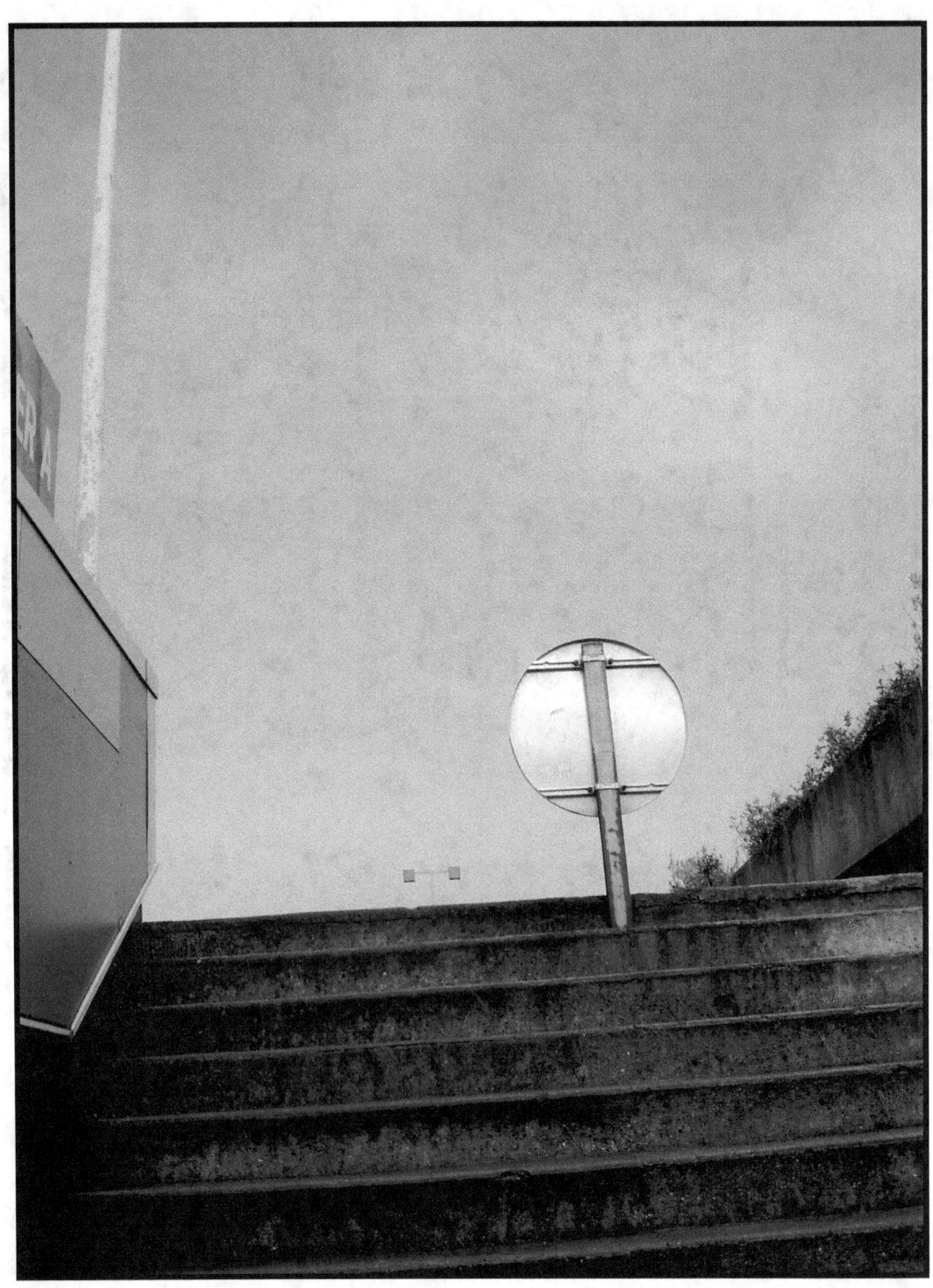

Vélizy (France) – April 2004

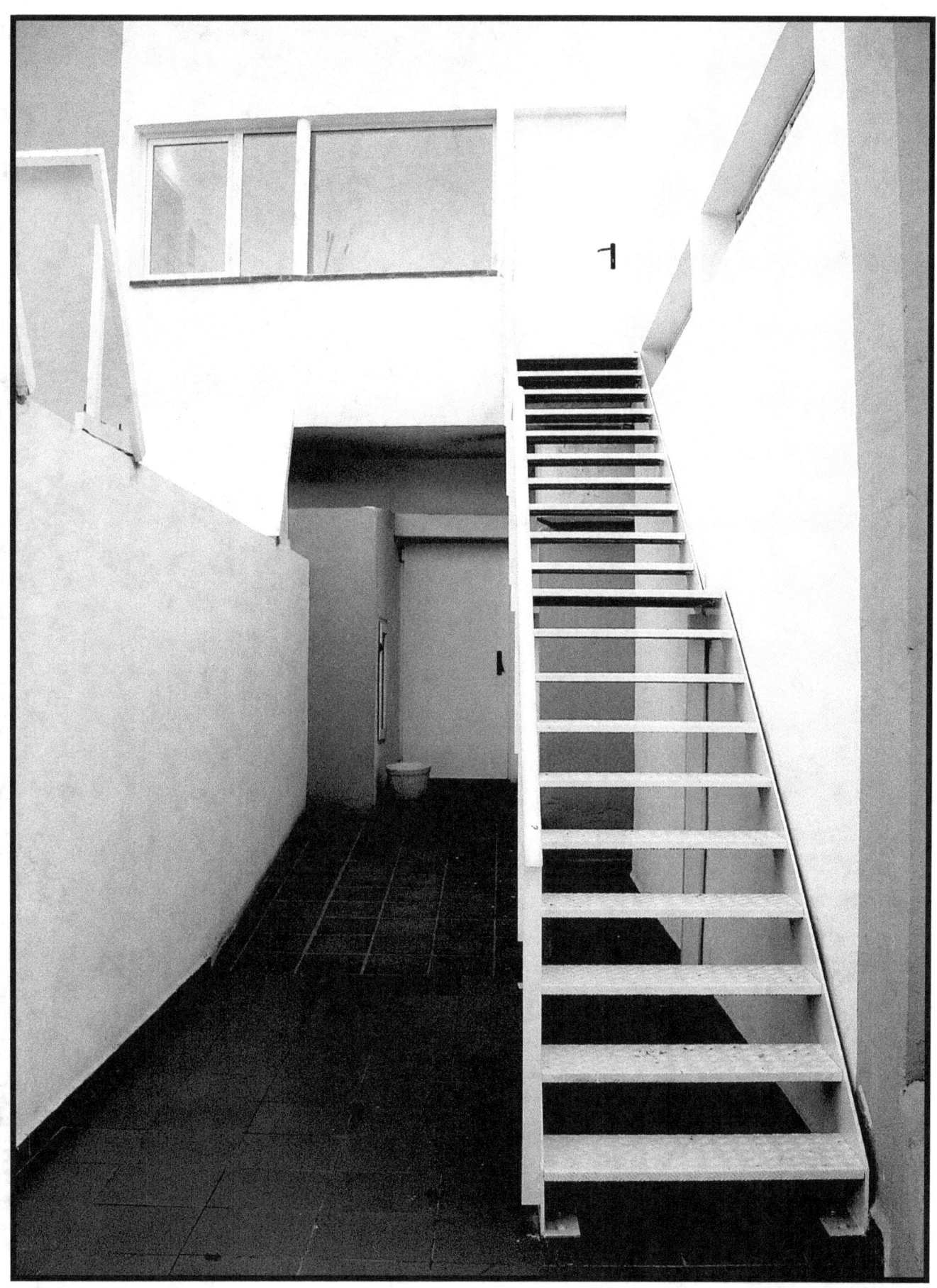

Marbella (Spain) – June 2004

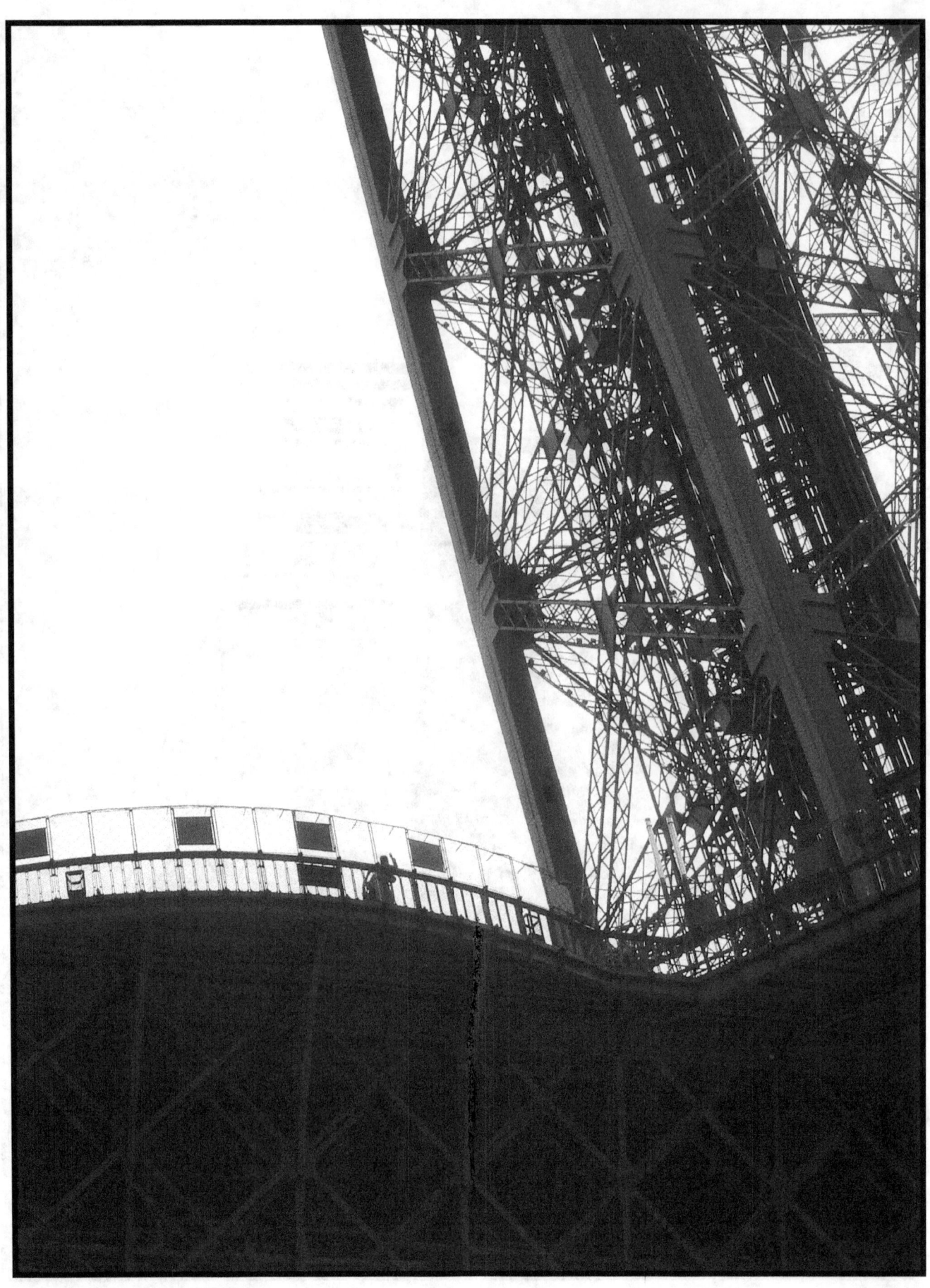

Paris (France) – April 2006

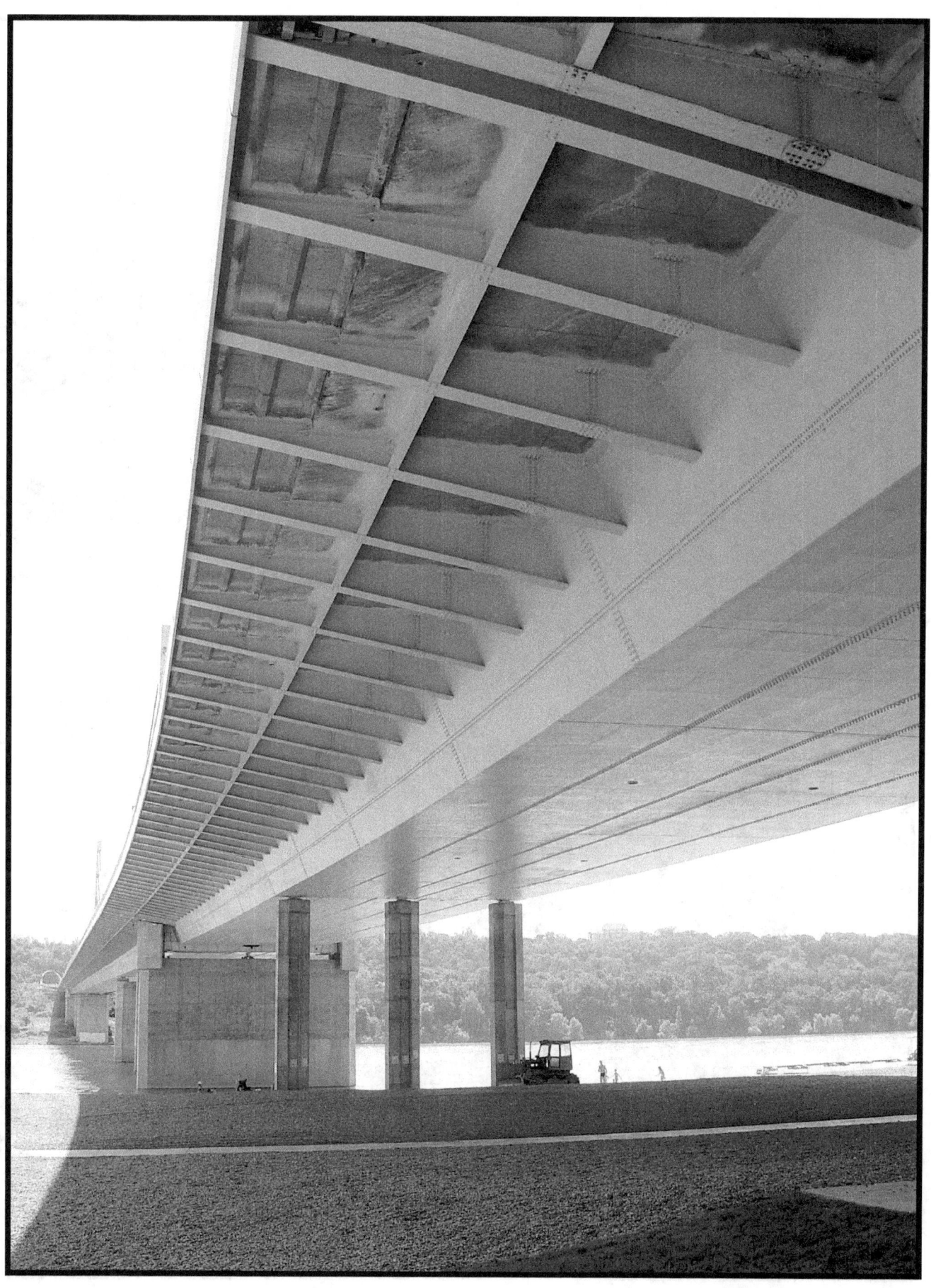

Novi Sad (Serbia) – August 2006

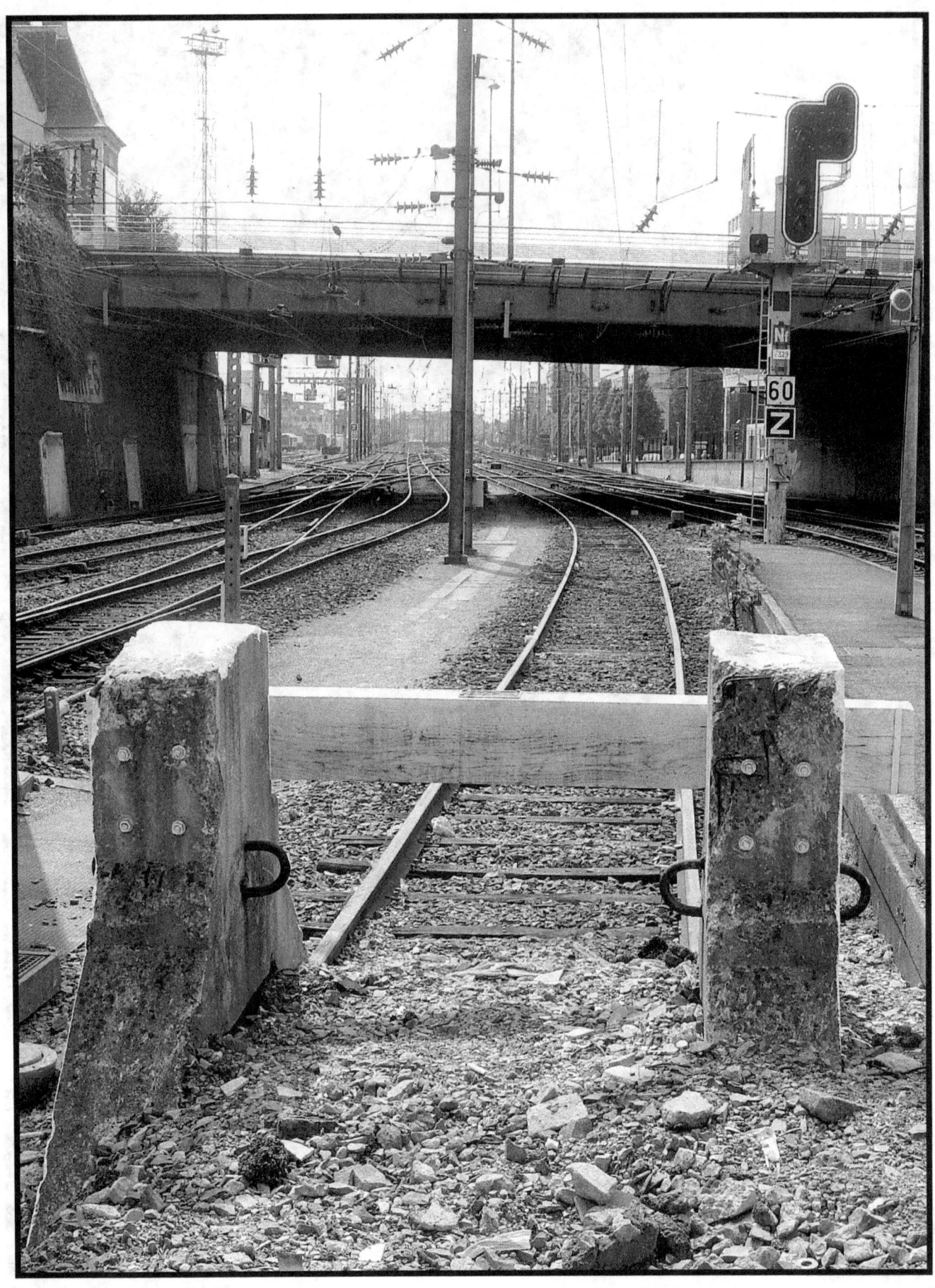

Rennes (France) – July 2006

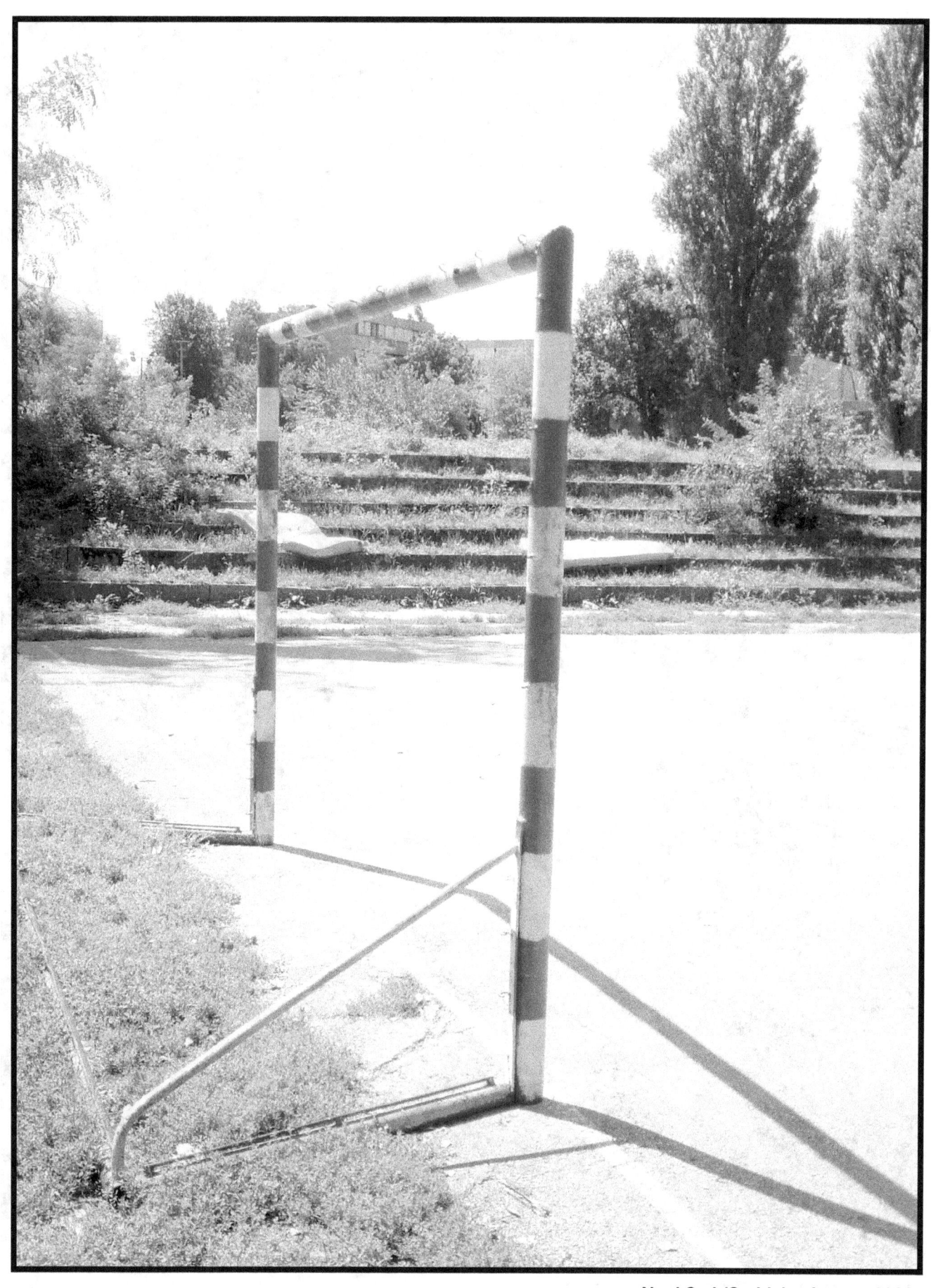

Novi Sad (Serbia) – August 2006

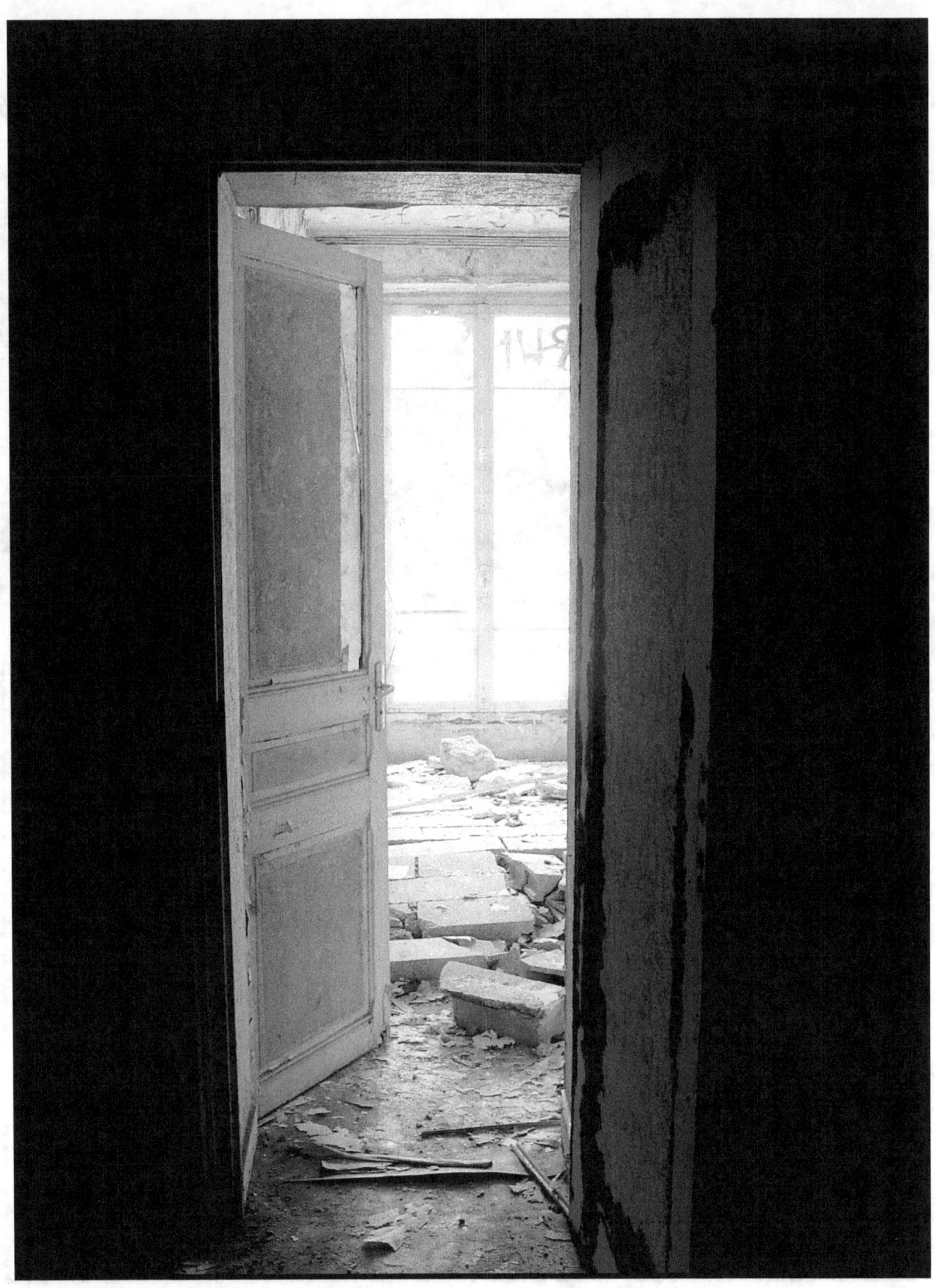

Issy-les-Moulineaux (France) – April 2006

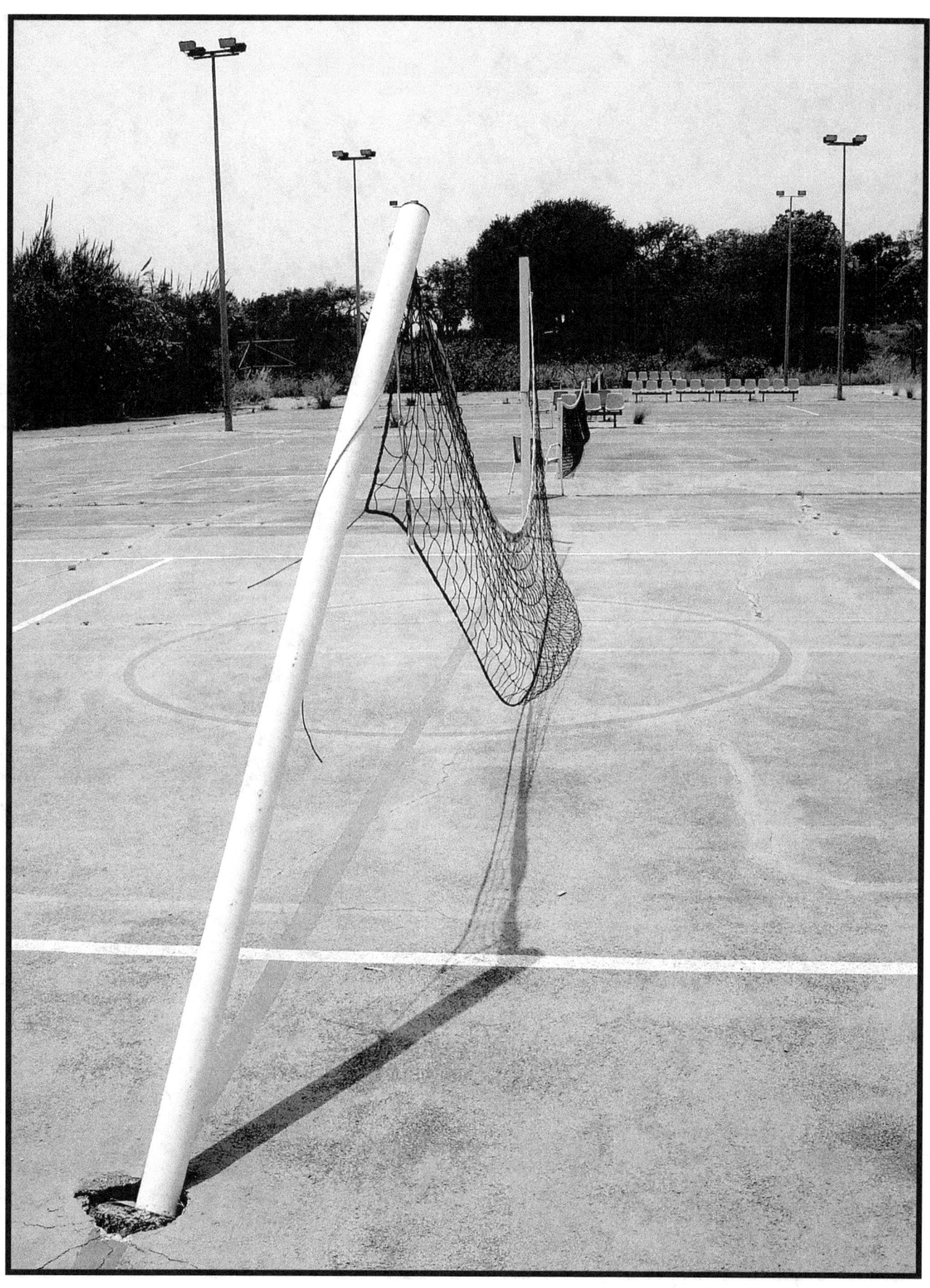

Marbella (Spain) – June 2004

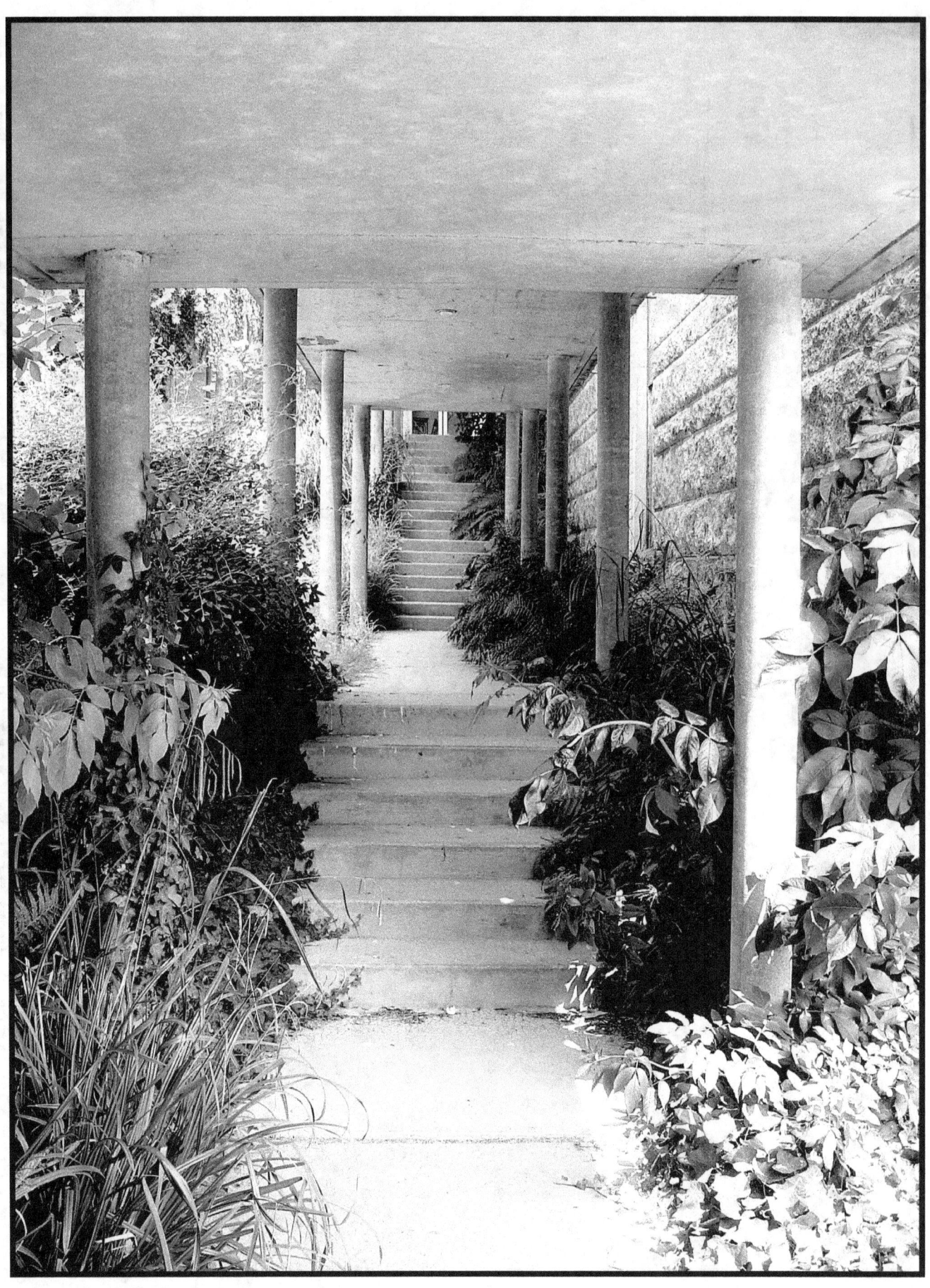

Rennes (France) – July 2006

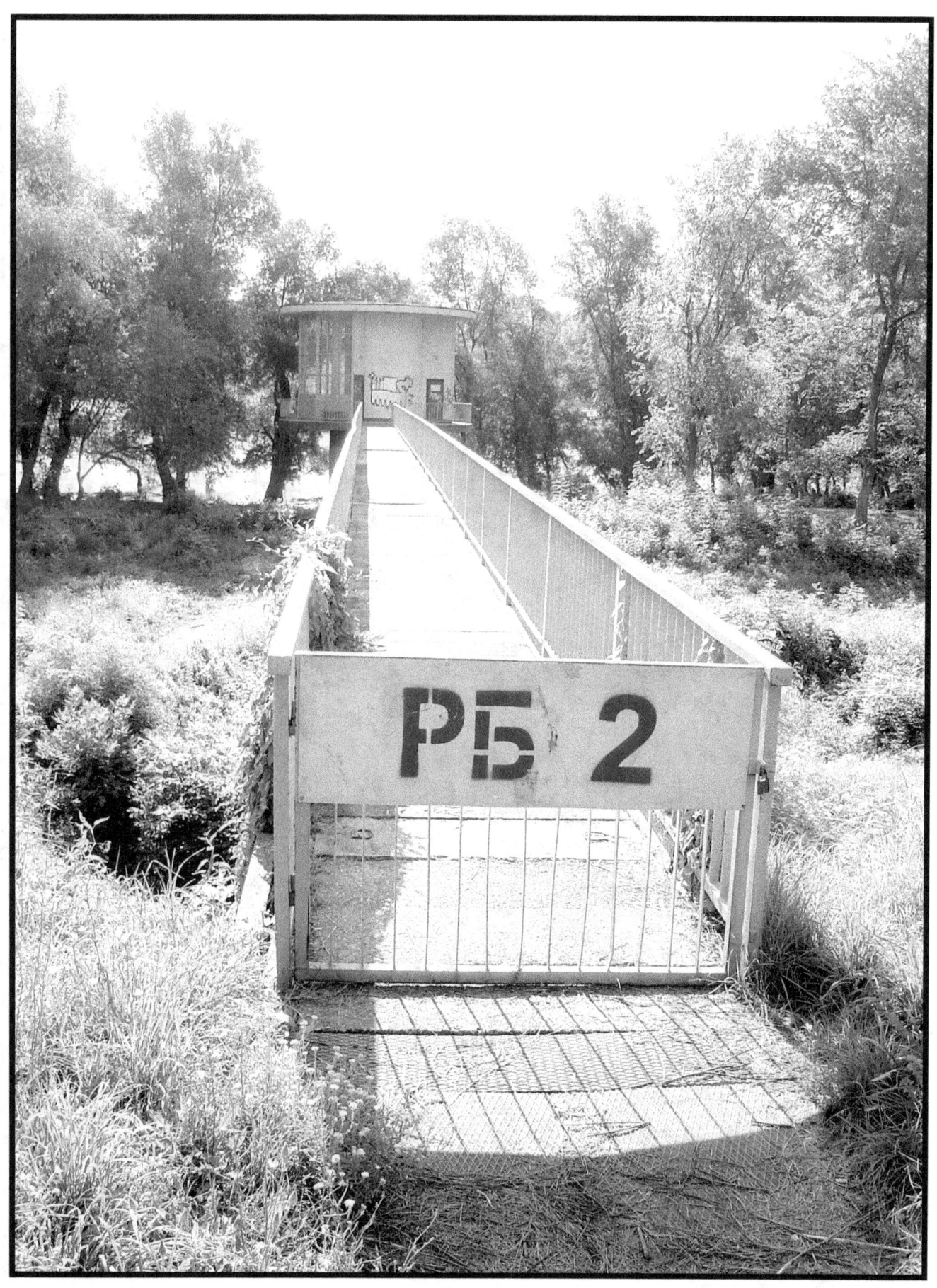

Novi Sad (Serbia) – August 2006

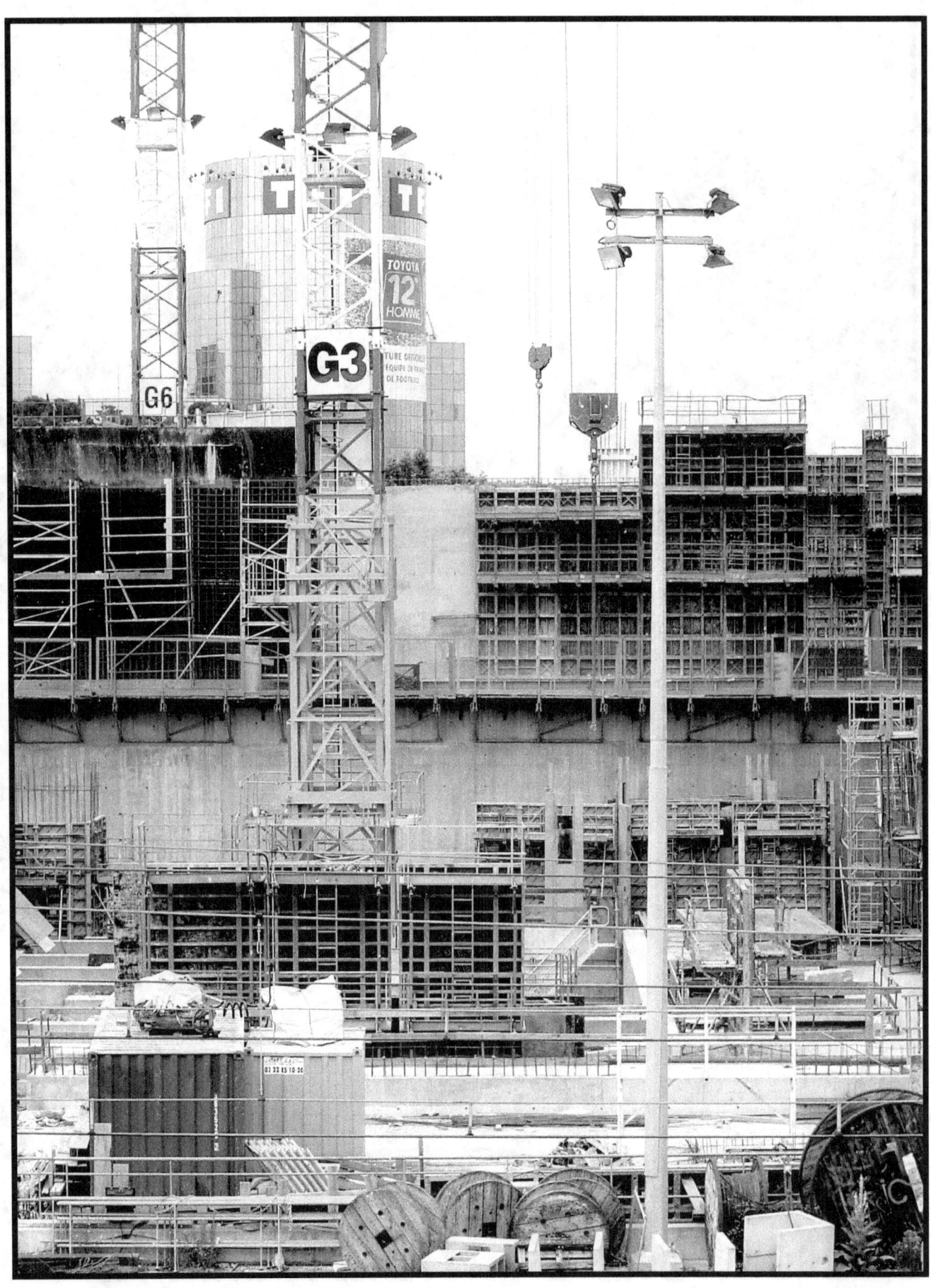

Issy-les-Moulineaux (France) – June 2006

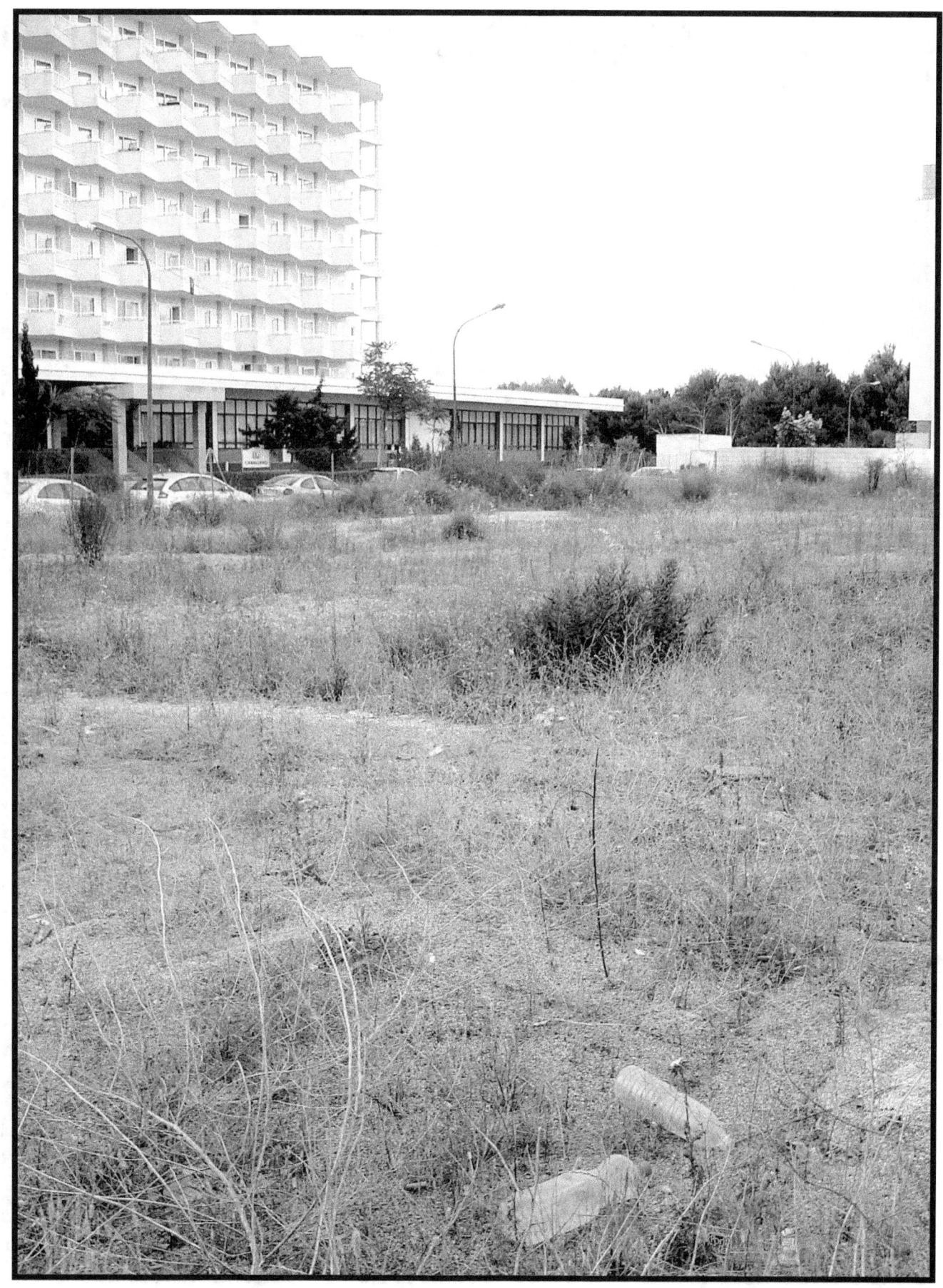

Mallorca (Spain) – June 2006

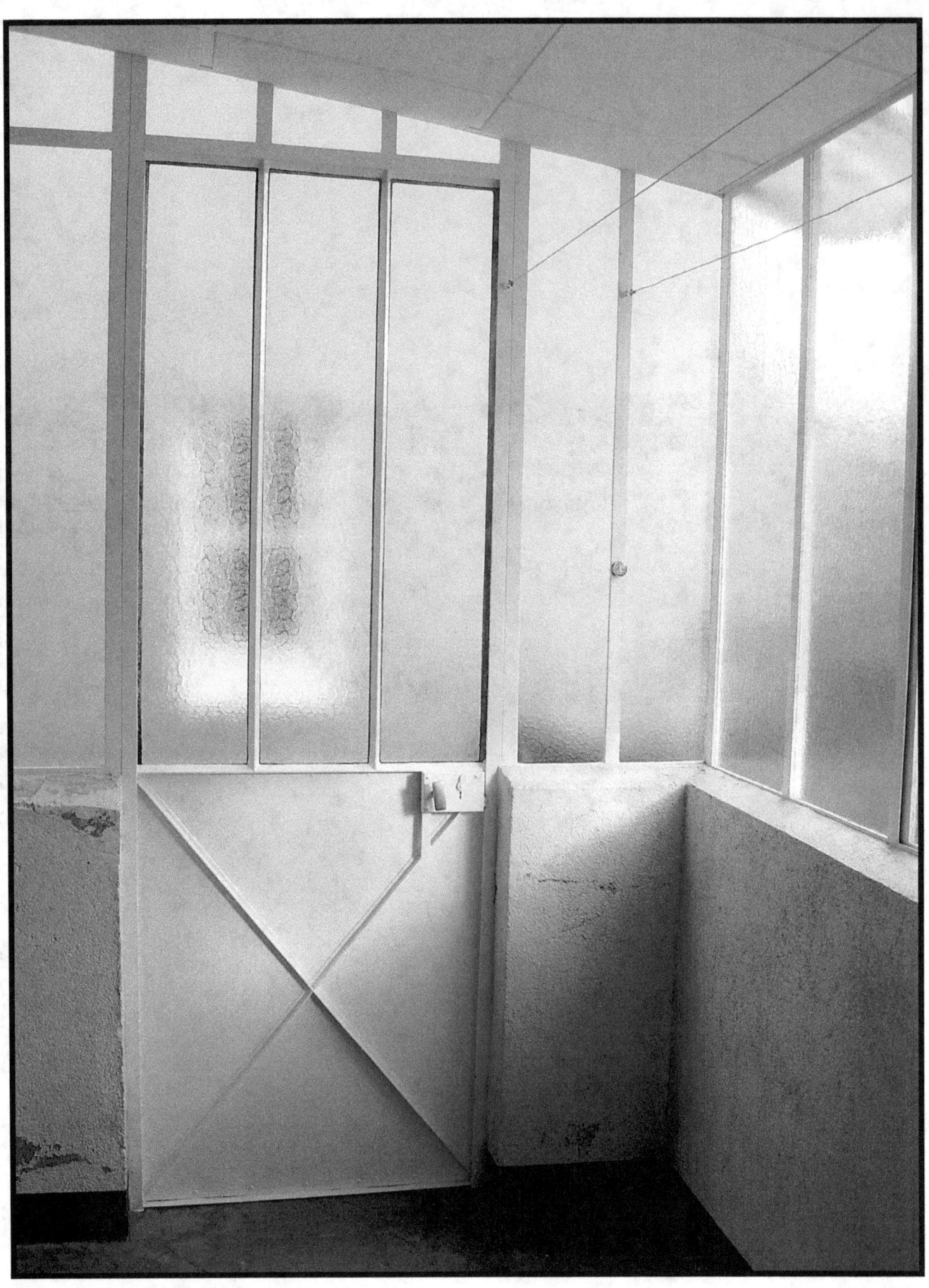

Rennes (France) – November 2004

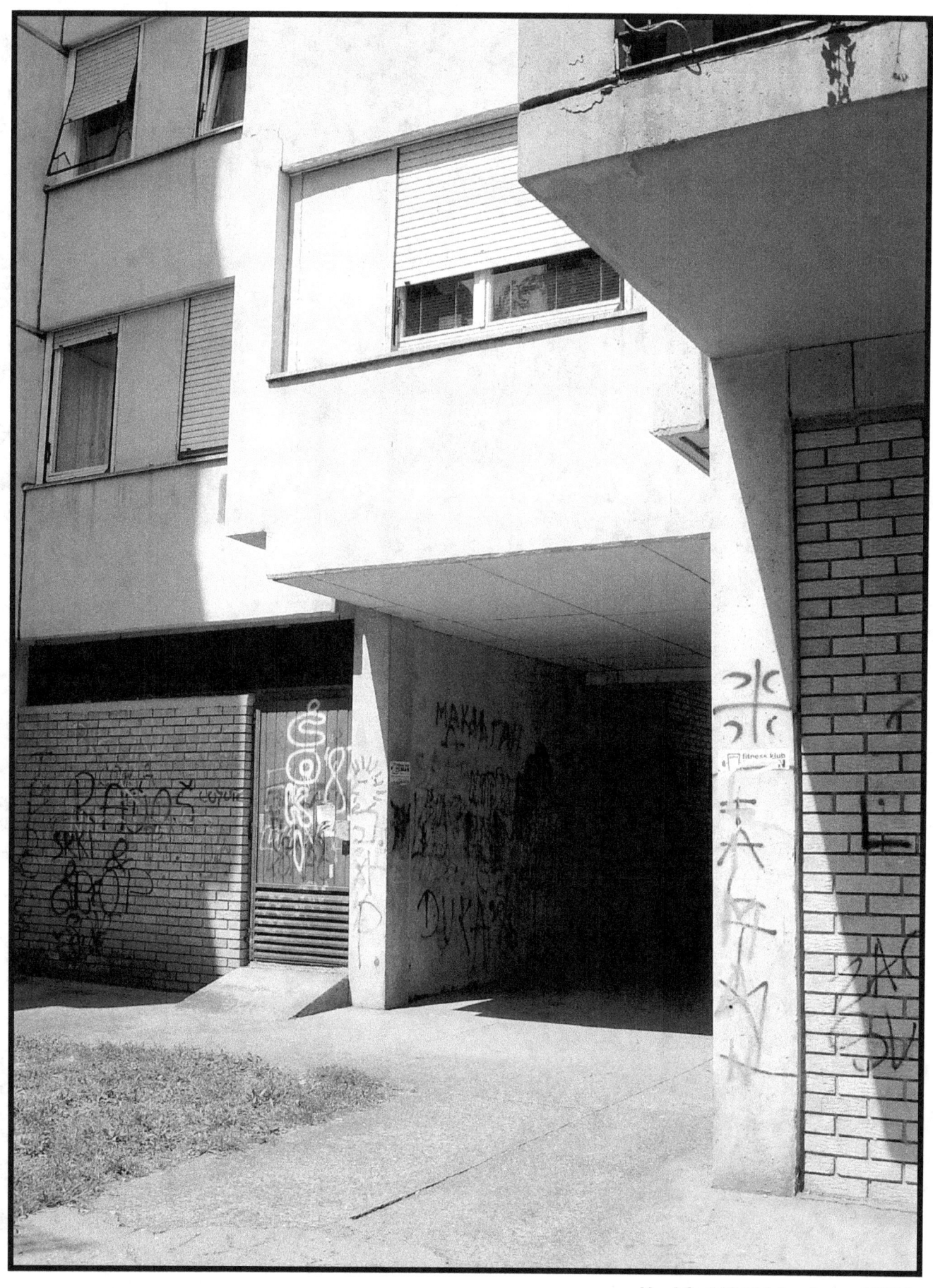

Novi Sad (Serbia) – August 2006

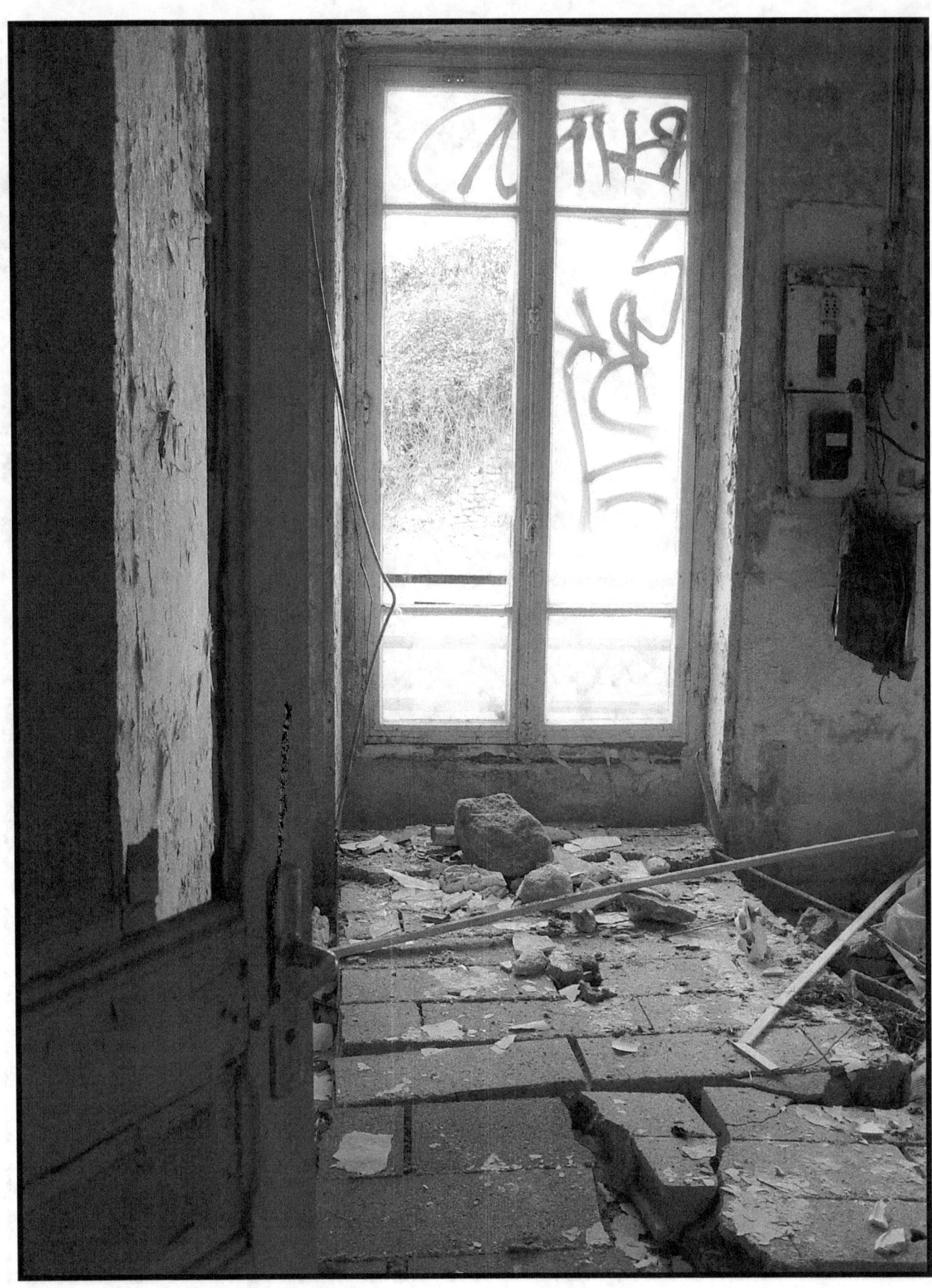

Issy-les-Moulineaux (France) – April 2006

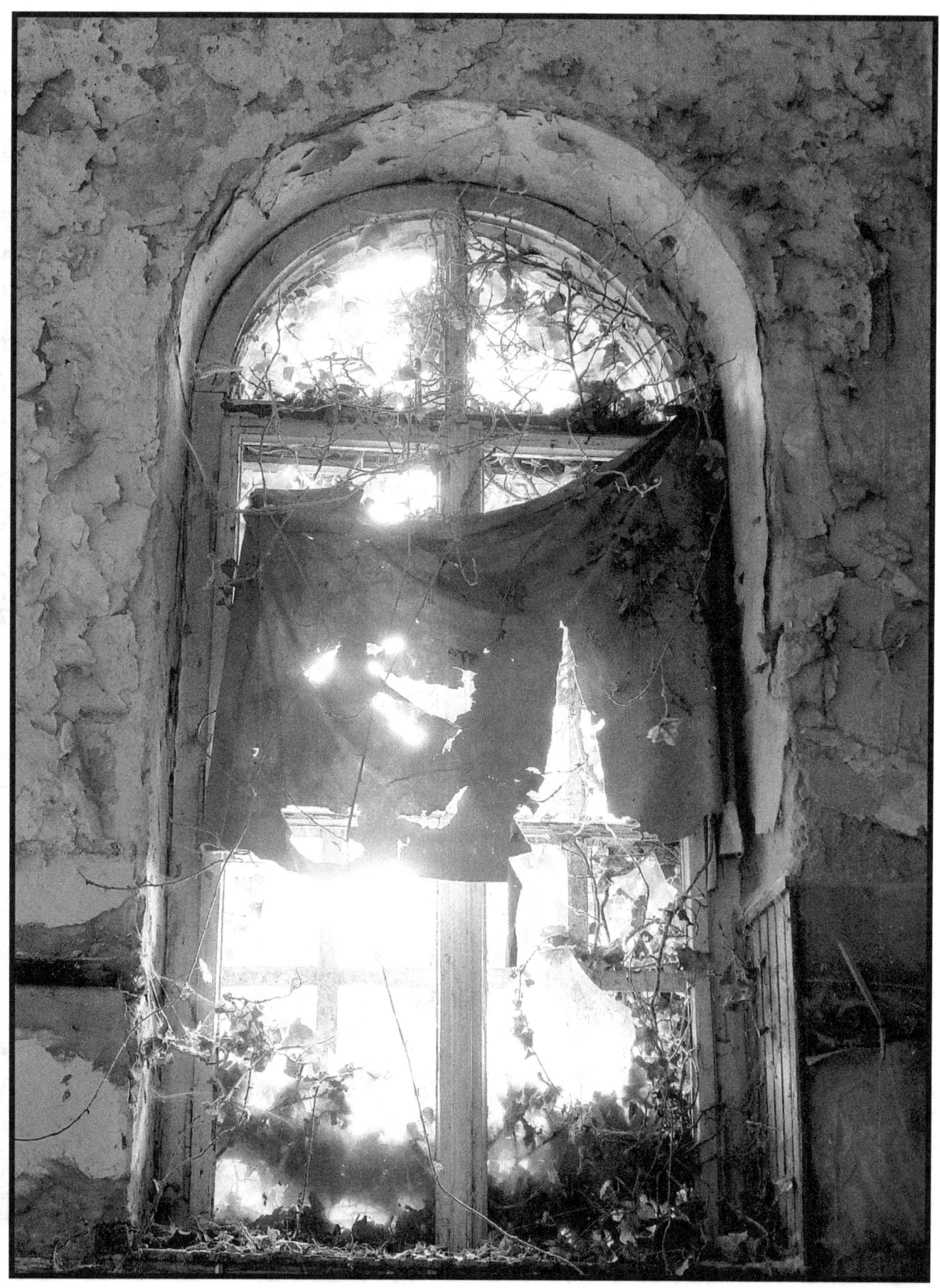

Novi Sad (Serbia) – August 2006

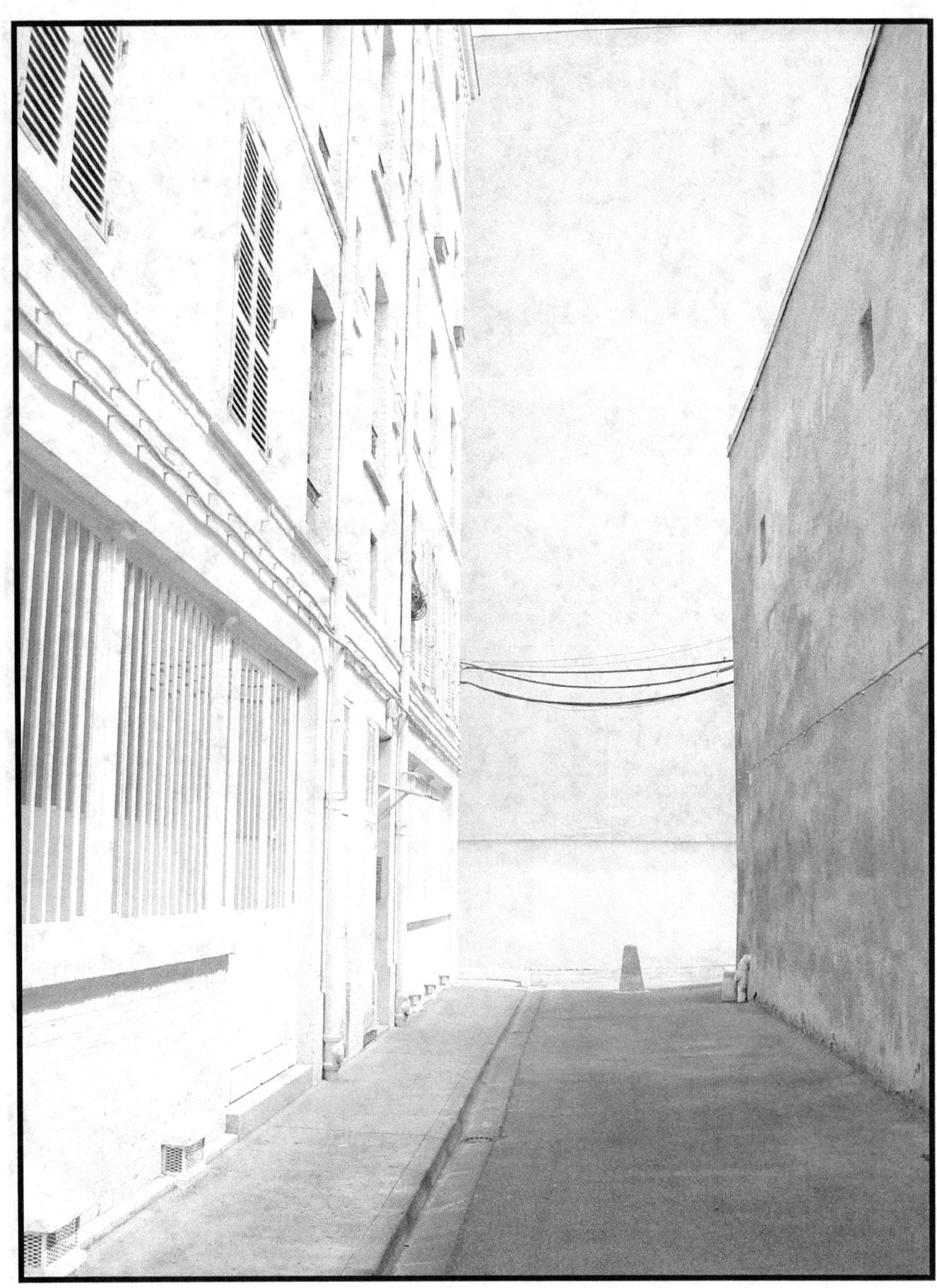

Paris (France) – April 2006

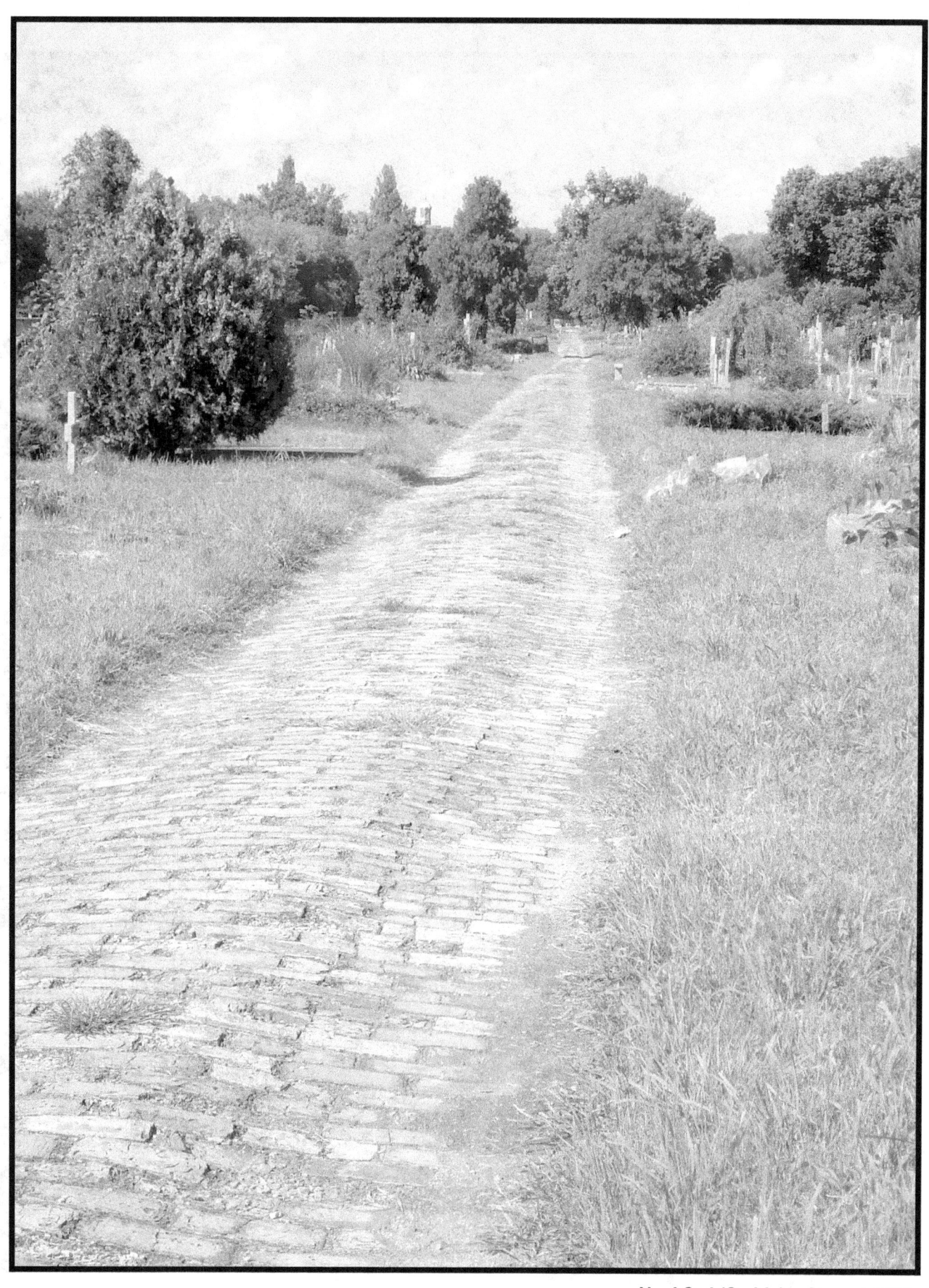

Novi Sad (Serbia) – August 2006

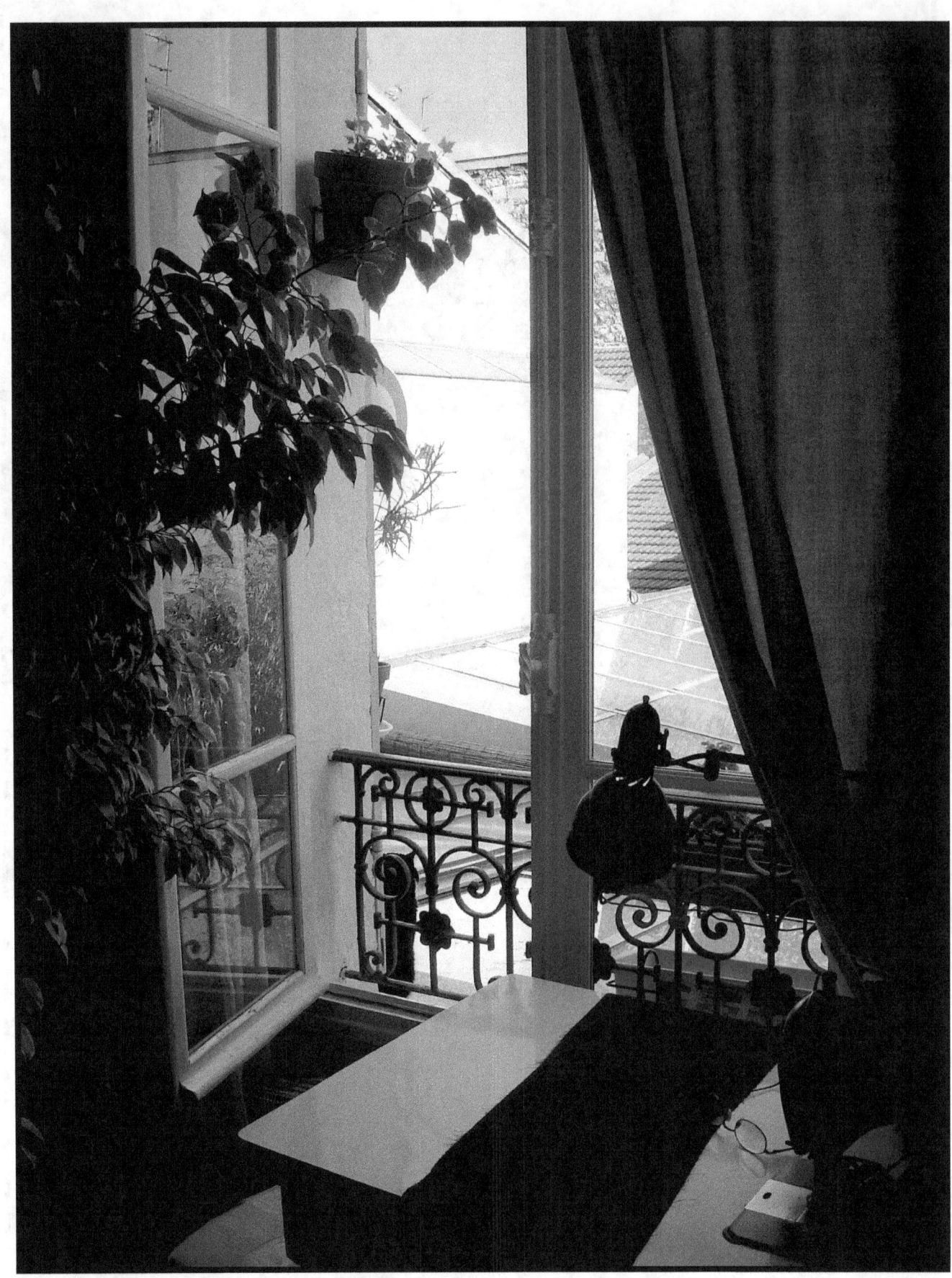

Paris (France) – April 2004

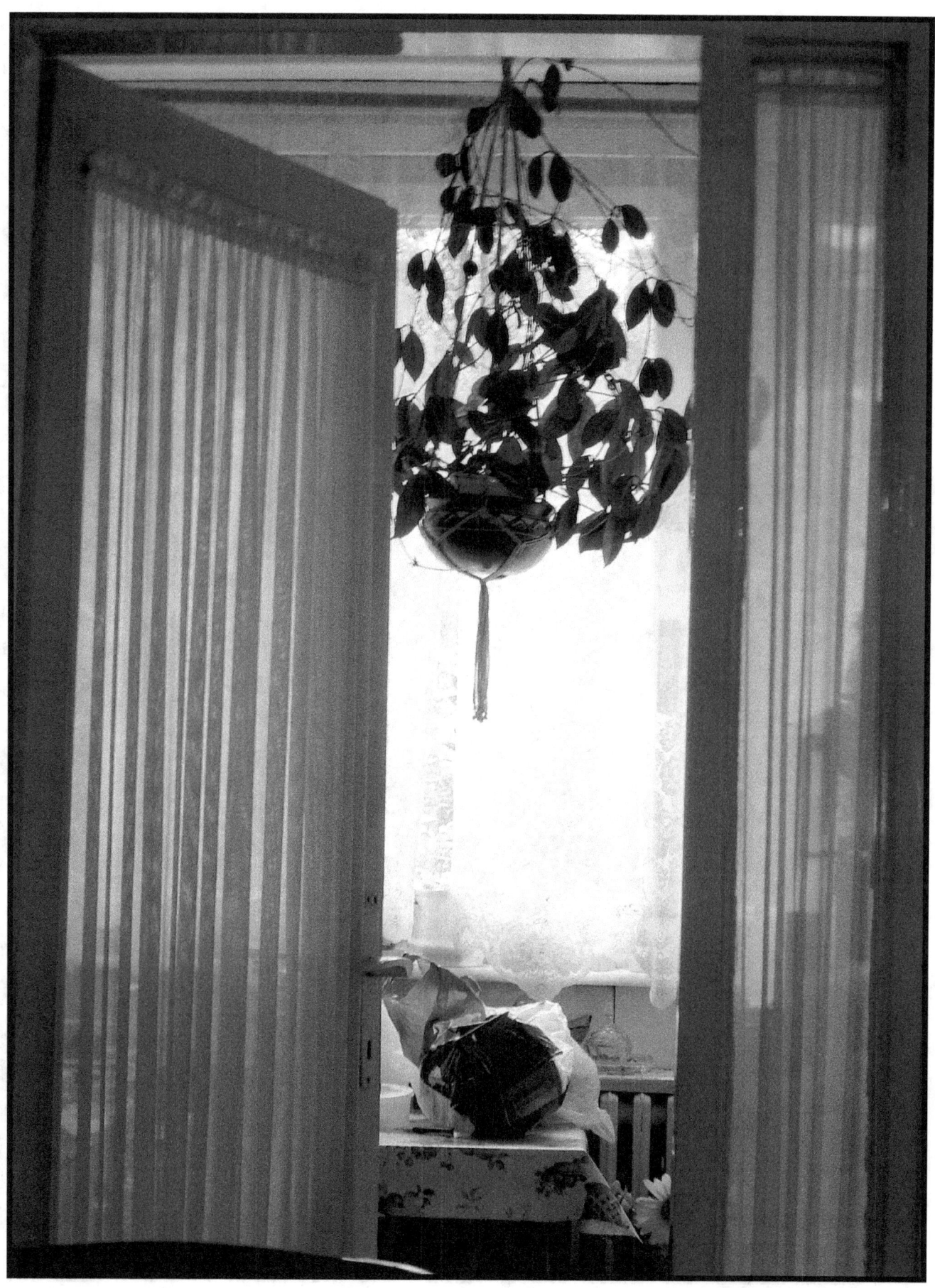

Novi Sad (Serbia) – August 2006

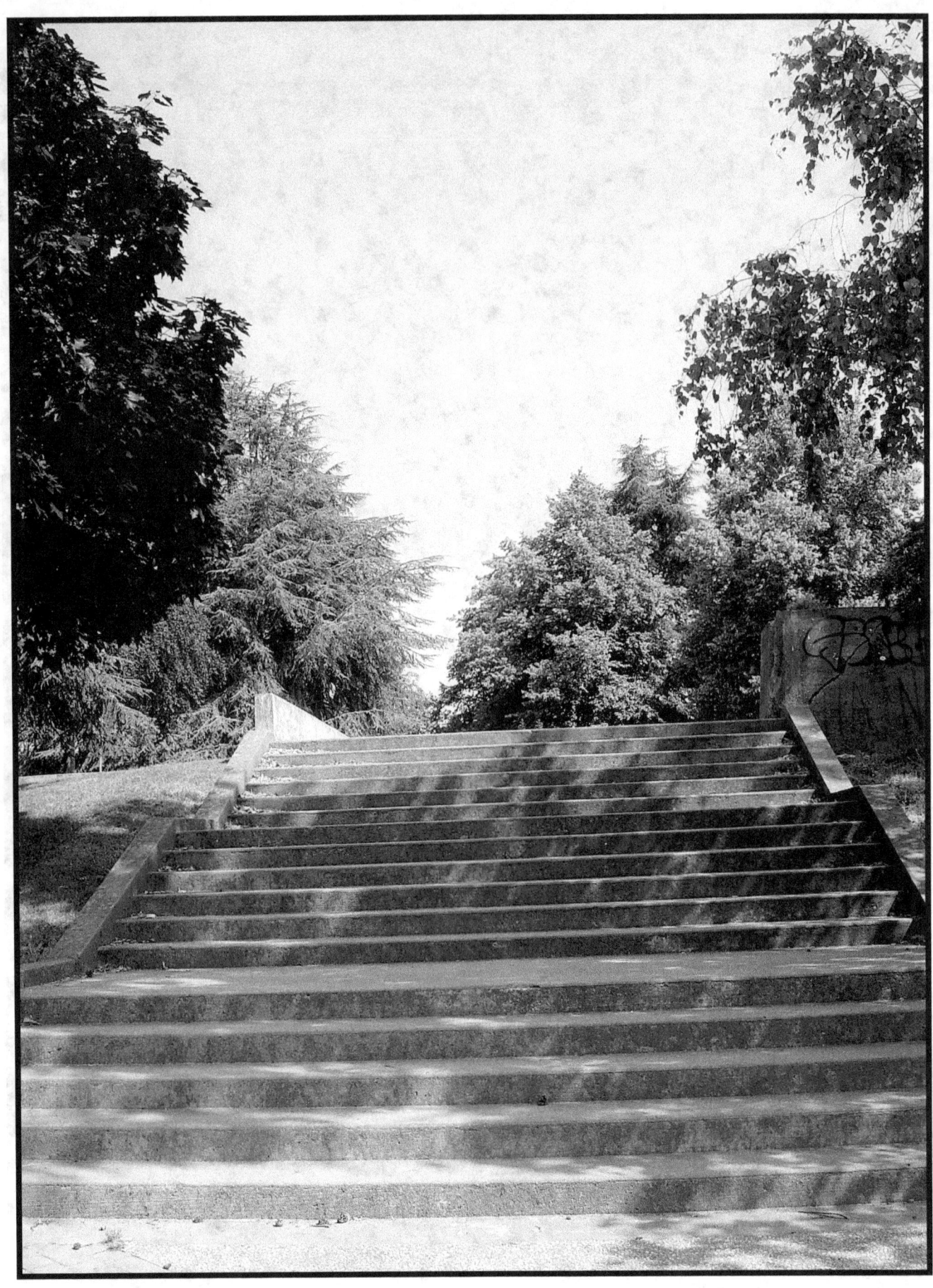

Rennes (France) – July 2006

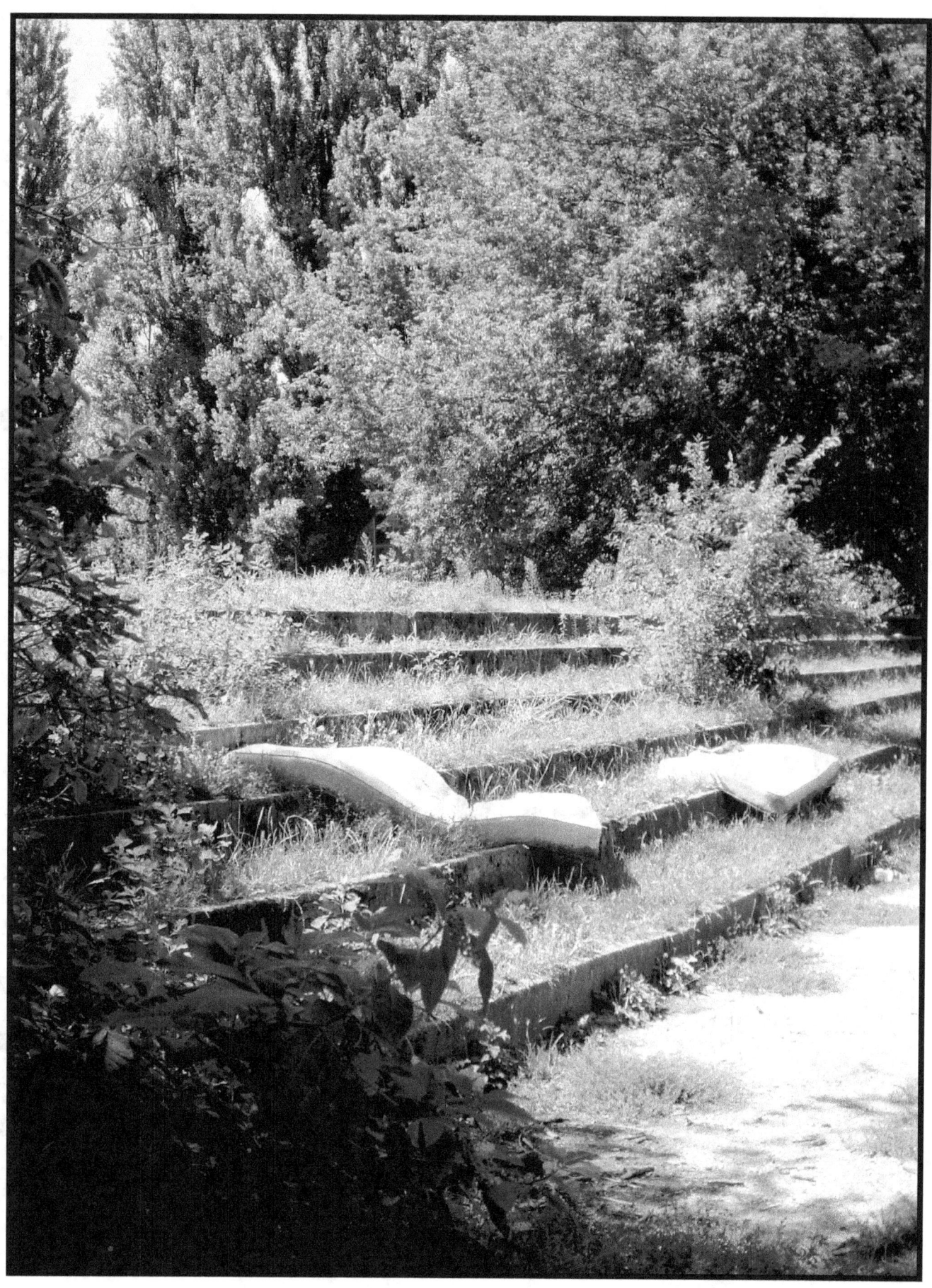

Novi Sad (Serbia) – August 2006

Issy-les-Moulineaux (France) – June 2006

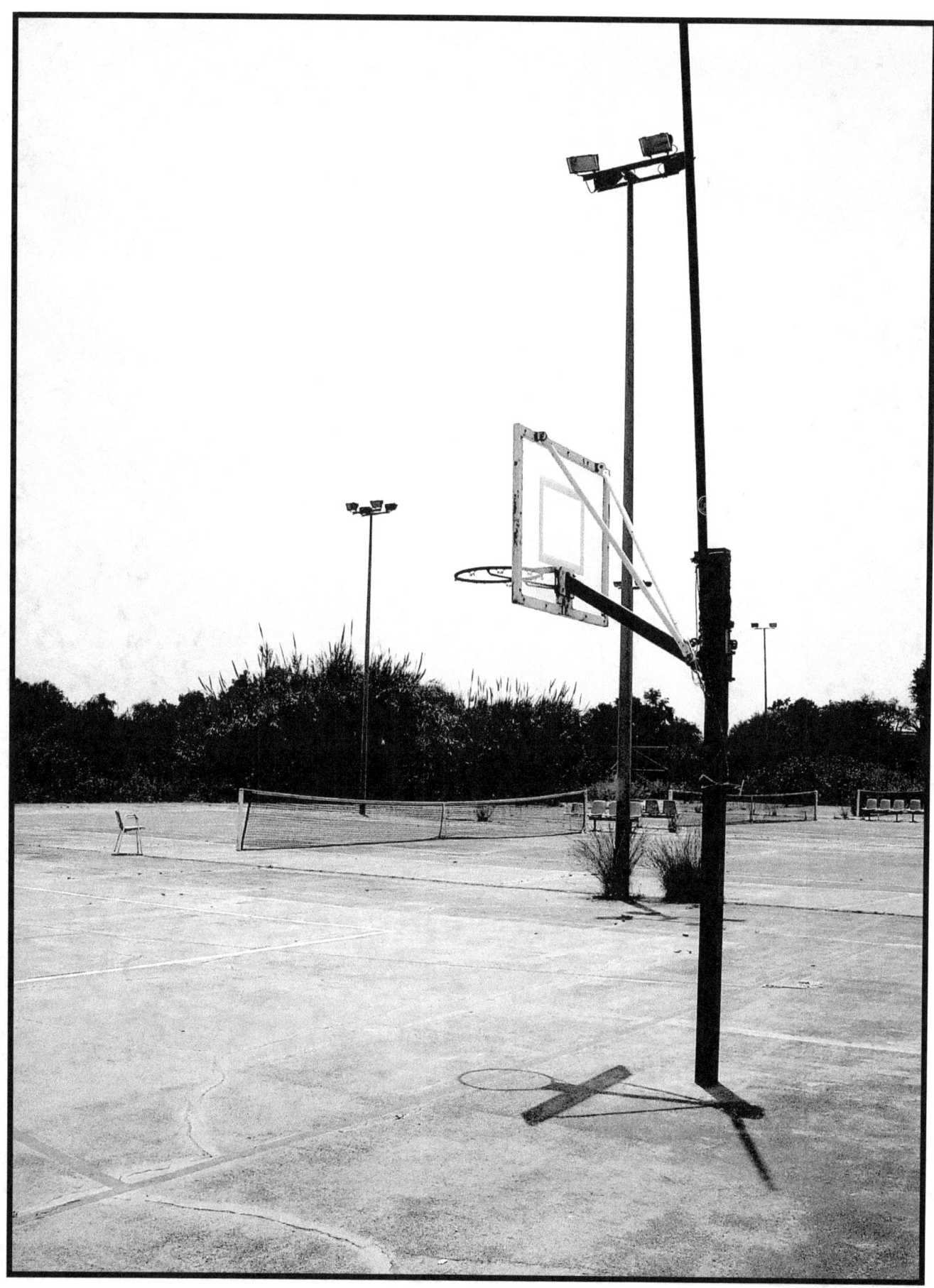

Marbella (spain) – June 2004

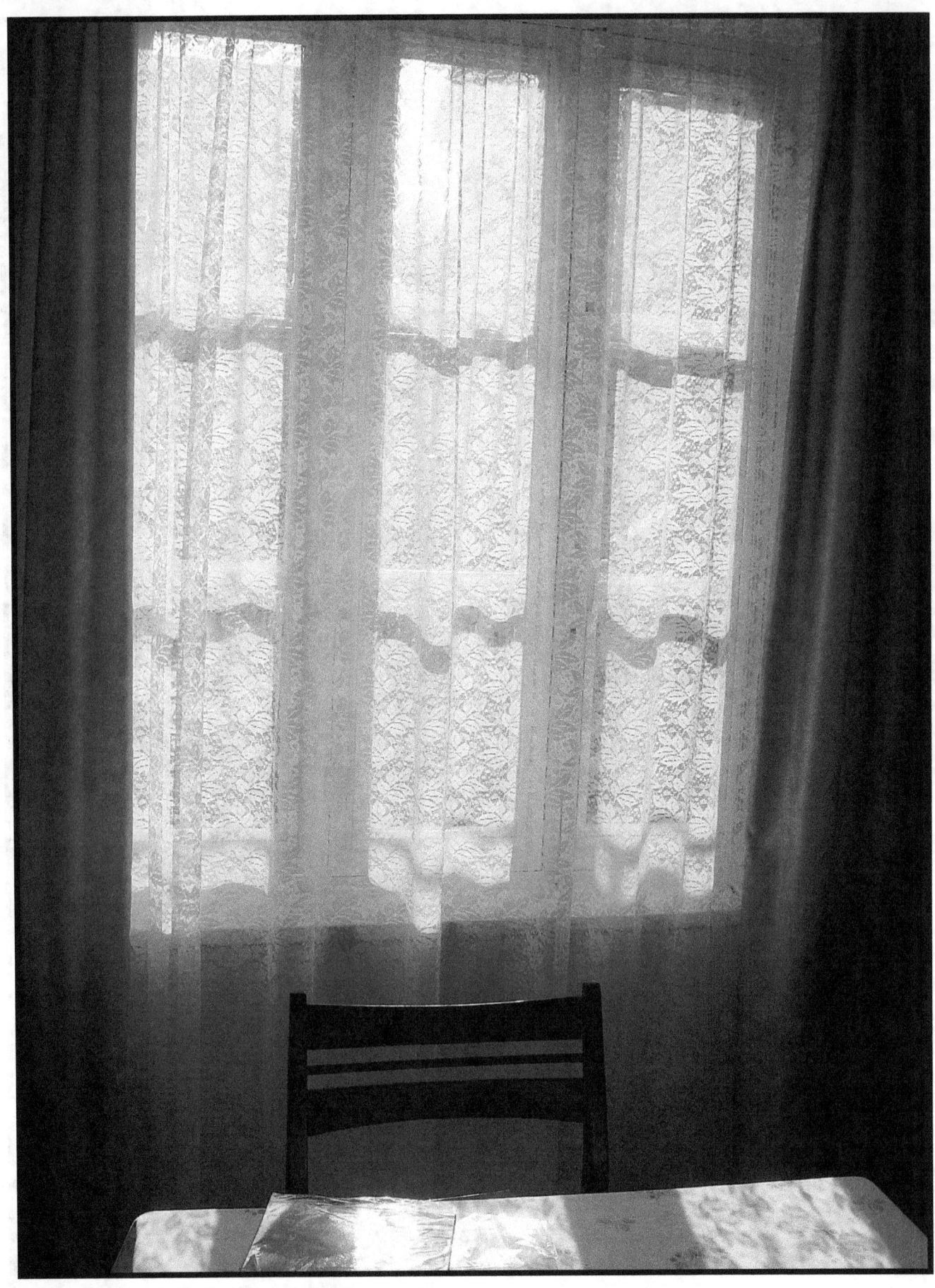

Bourg-la-Reine (France) – October 2005

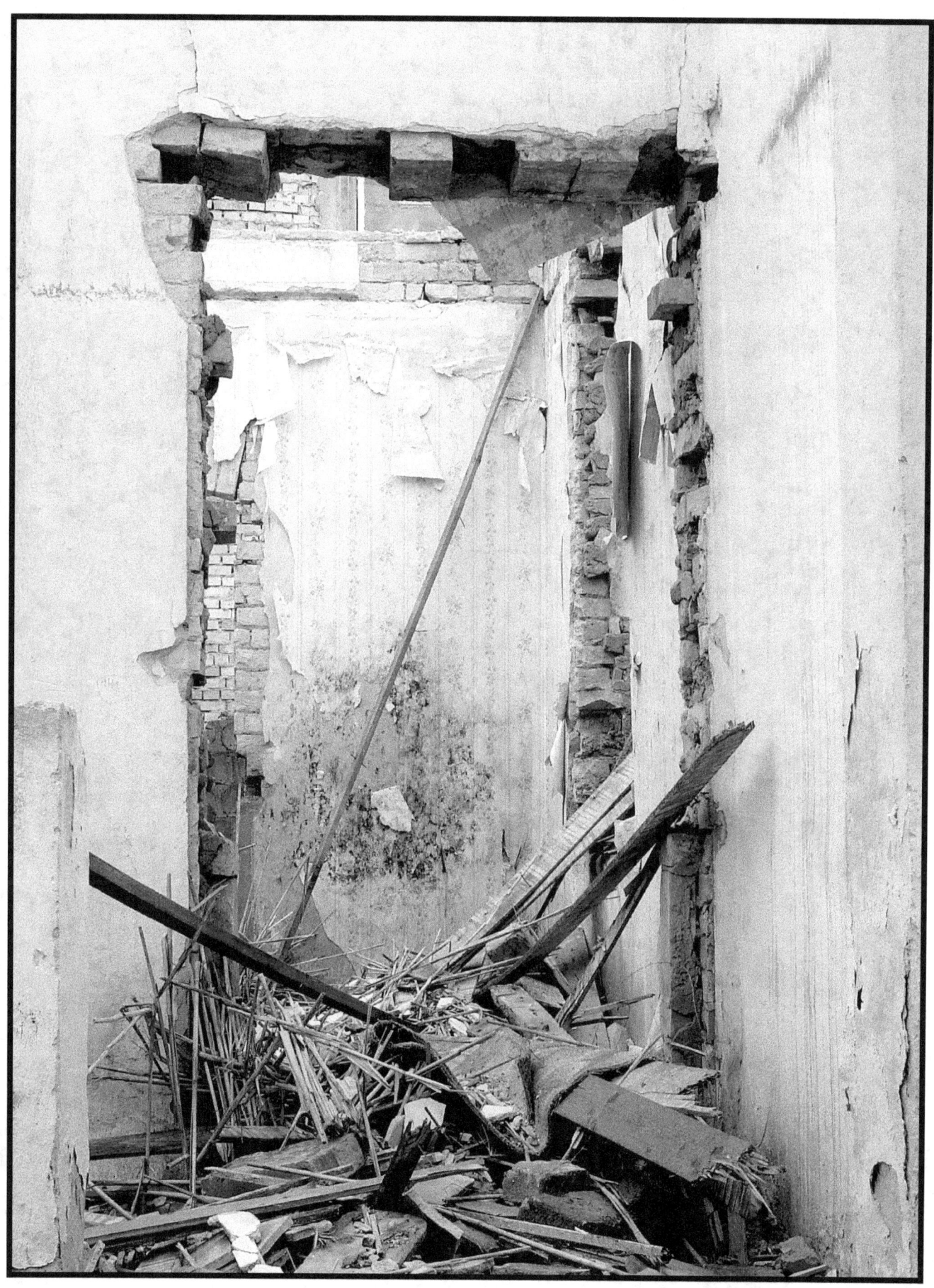

Novi Sad (Serbia) – August 2006

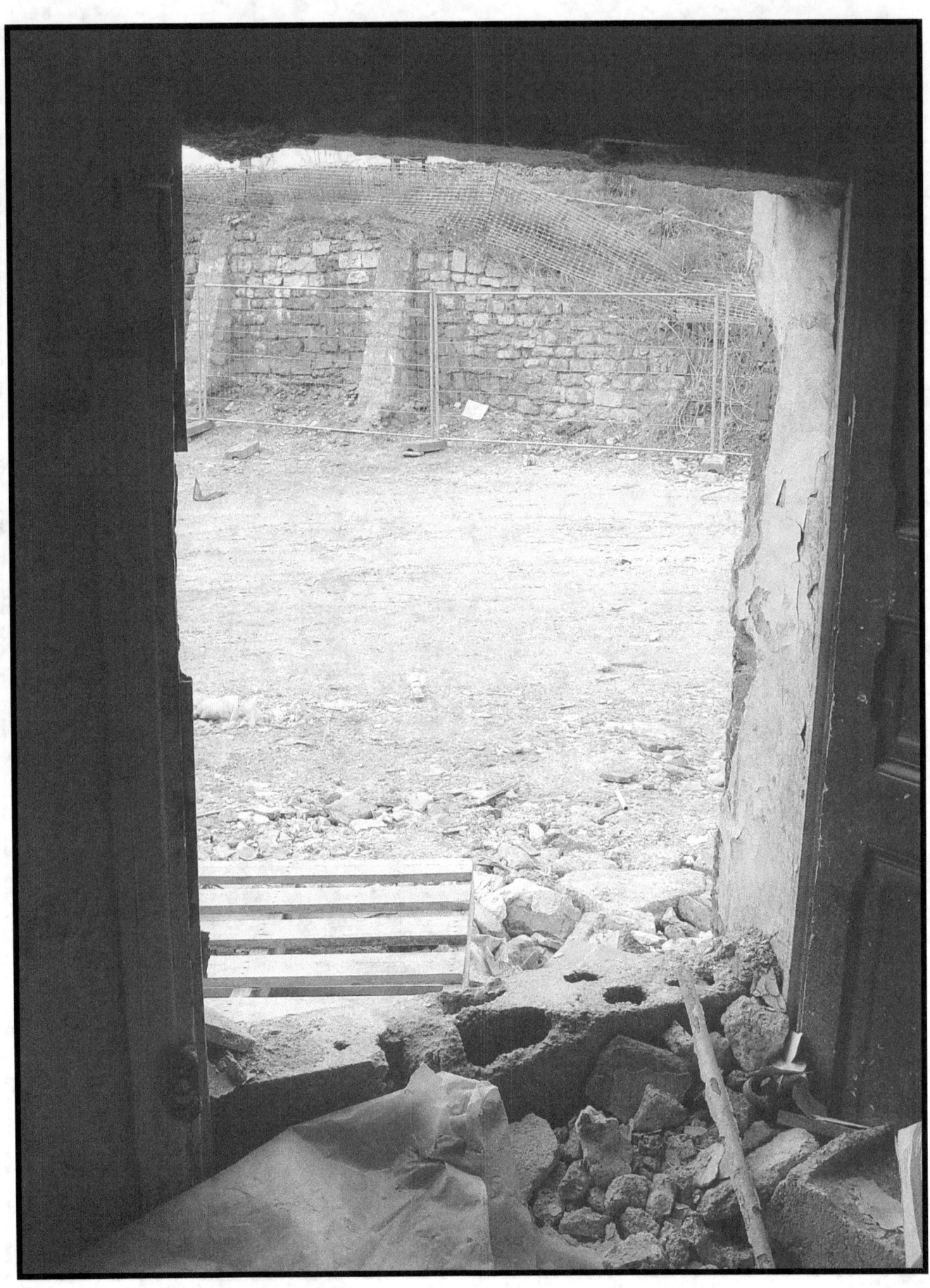

Issy-les-Moulineaux (France) – April 2006

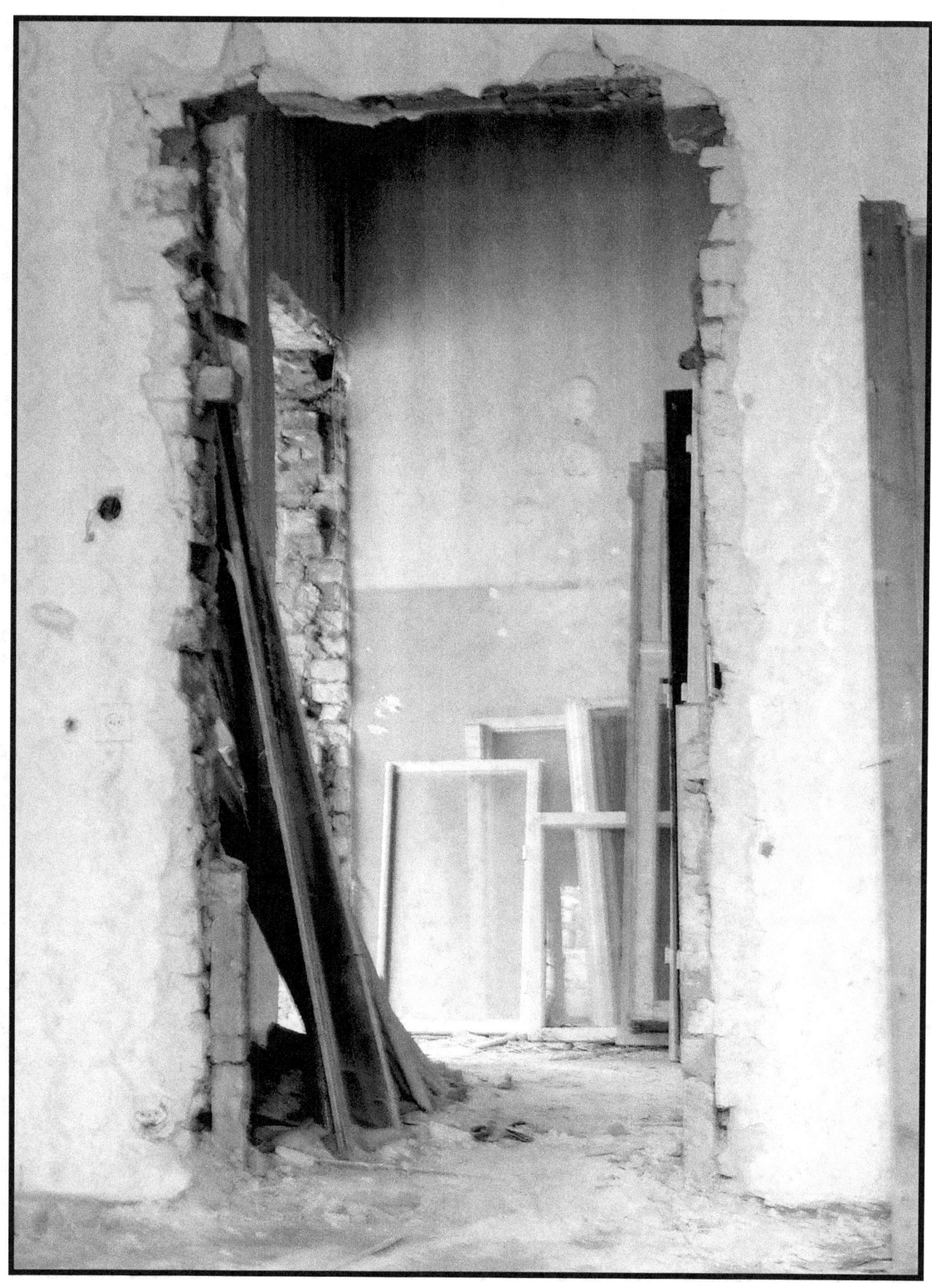

Novi Sad (Serbia) – August 2006

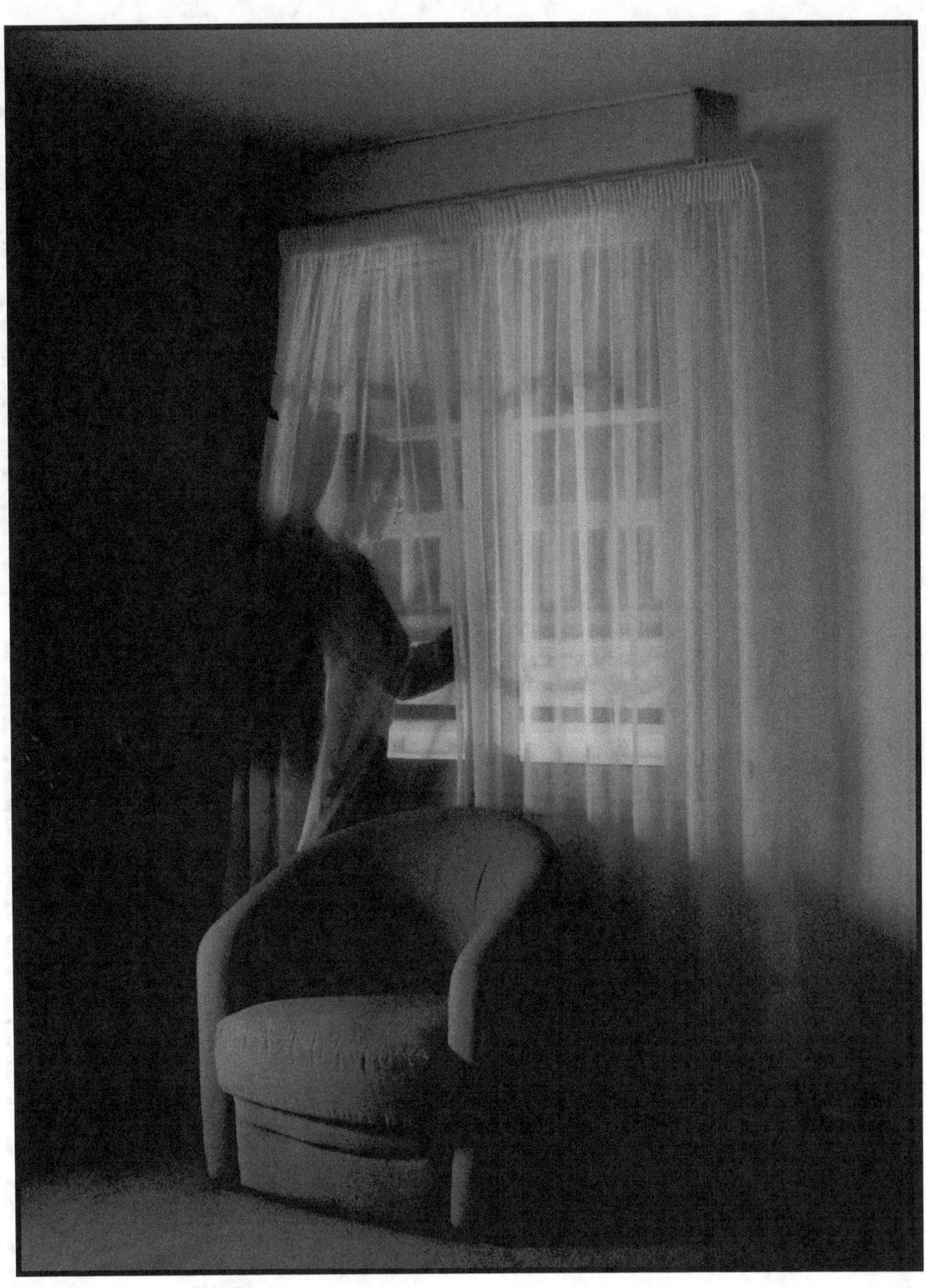

Paris (France) – June 2006

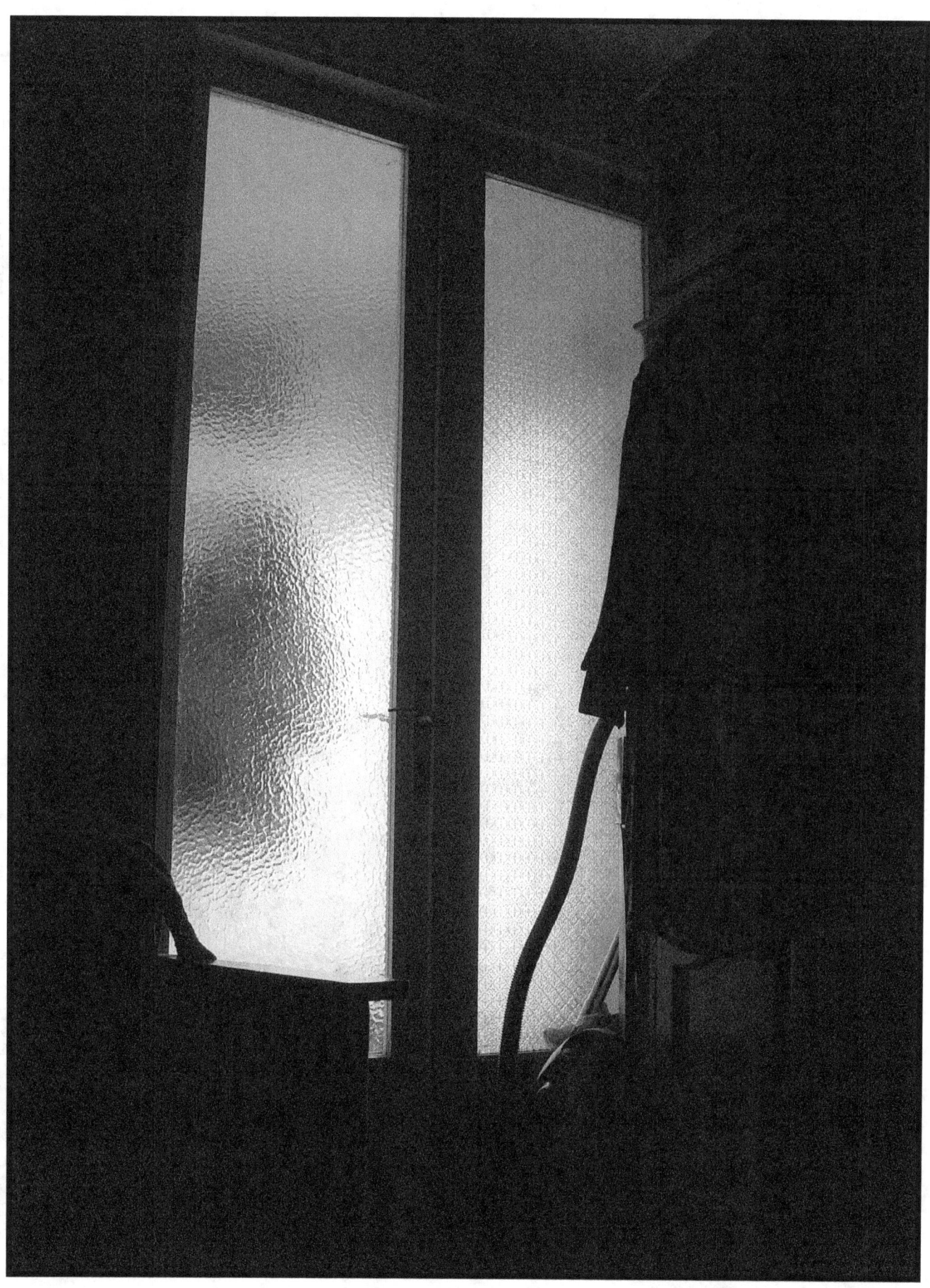

Novi Sad (Serbia) – August 2006

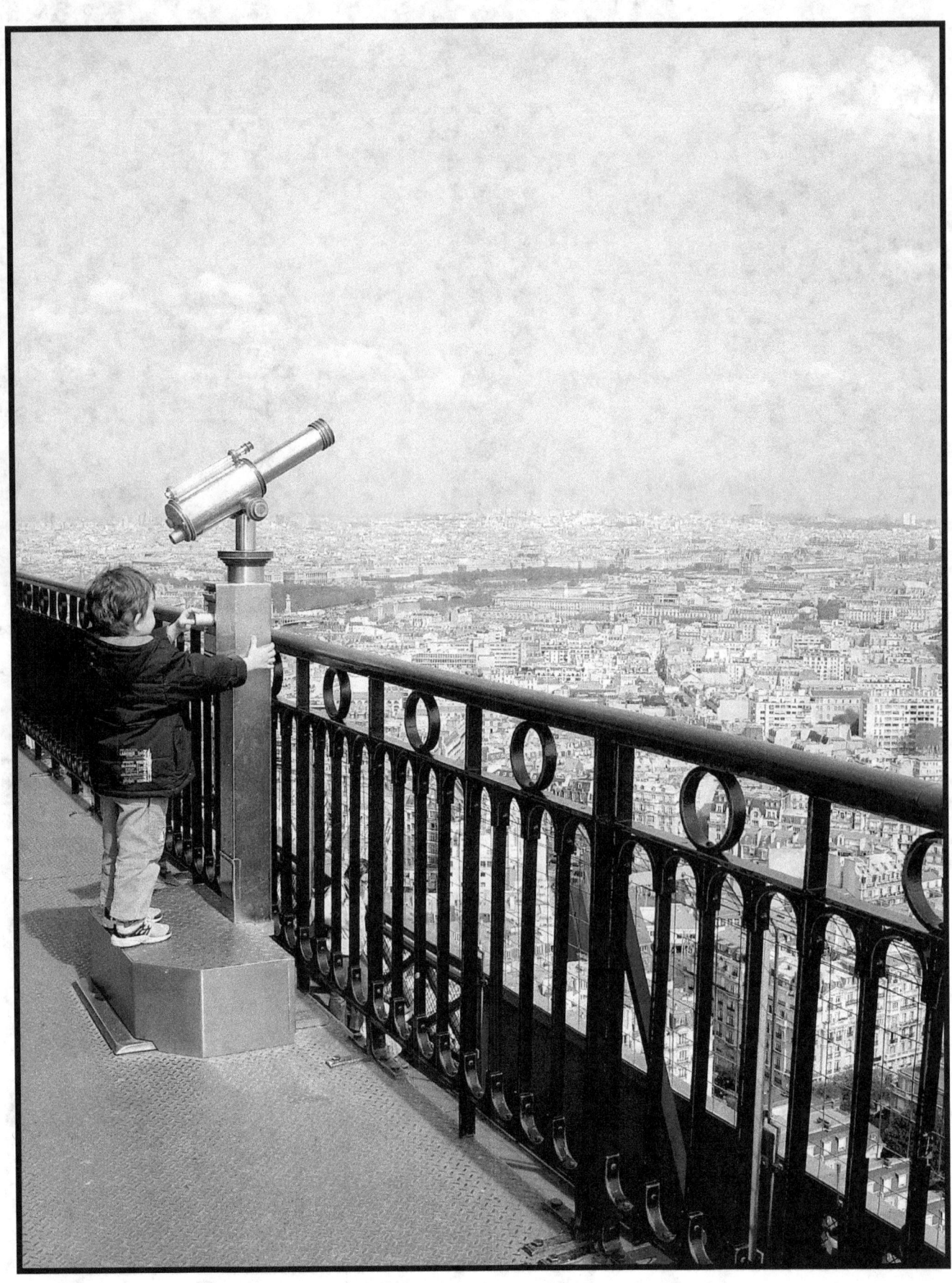

Paris (France) – April 2006

www.ingramcontent.com/pod-product-compliance
Lightning Source LLC
Chambersburg PA
CBHW081745220526
45468CB00008B/2253